SLAVERY IN AMERICAN HISTORY

THE RISE AND FALL OF AMERICAN SLAVERY
FREEDOM DENIED, FREEDOM GAINED

TIM MCNEESE

FOREWORD BY SERIES ADVISOR
DR. HENRY LOUIS GATES, JR.

Enslow Publishers, Inc.

40 Industrial Road   PO Box 38
Box 398   Aldershot
Berkeley Heights, NJ 07922   Hants GU12 6BP
USA   UK

http://www.enslow.com

Library of Congress Cataloging-in-Publication Data

McNeese, Tim.
    The rise and fall of American slavery: freedom denied, freedom gained / Tim McNeese.
      v. cm.—(Slavery in American history)
    Includes bibliographical references and index.
    Contents: The slave trade and the Middle Passage—Slavery in the British colonies—Slavery
and the American Revolution—Slavery and King Cotton—Abolition and emancipation.
    ISBN 0-7660-2156-4
    1. Slavery—United States—History—Juvenile literature. 2. Antislavery movements—United
States—History—Juvenile literature. 3. African Americans—History—To 1863—Juvenile
literature. [1. Slavery—United States—History. 2. Antislavery movements. 3. African
Americans—History—To 1863. 4. United States—History—To 1775. 5. United States—
History—1775–1865.] I. Title. II. Series.
    E441.M44 2004
    973'.0496—dc22

                                       2003013459

Printed in the United States of America

10 9 8 7 6 5 4 3 2 1

To Our Readers: We have done our best to make sure all Internet Addresses in this book were
active and appropriate when we went to press. However, the author and the publisher have no
control over and assume no liability for the material available on those Internet sites or on other
Web sites they may link to. Any comments or suggestions can be sent by e-mail to
comments@enslow.com or to the address on the back cover.

Illustration Credits: © The Art Archive, p. 14; Courtesy Library of Congress, reproduced
from the *Dictionary of American Portraits*, published by Dover Publications, Inc., in
1967, p. 95; Culver Pictures, pp. 48, 62; Engraving by H. B. Hall and Sons, reproduced
from the *Dictionary of American Portraits*, published by Dover Publications, Inc.,
p. 105; Enslow Publishers, Inc., p. 24, 46, 83, 94; The Granger Collection, p. 50; Jane
Reed/Harvard News Office, p. 5; The John Carter Brown Library at Brown University,
p. 26; Kansas State Historical Society, p. 100; Mary Evans Picture Library, p. 36; National
Archives and Records Administration, p. 59, 81; Reproduced from the Collections of
the Library of Congress, pp. 1, 3, 6–7, 20, 30, 61, 72, 78, 91, 109; Reproduced from the
Dictionary of American Portraits, published by Dover Publications, Inc., in 1967, p. 89;
Snark/Art Resource, NY, p. 75.

Cover Illustration: Reproduced from the Collections of the Library of Congress.

⤞ Contents ⤝

⌒═⌒

FOREWORD BY SERIES ADVISOR
HENRY LOUIS GATES, JR. 4

1 THE STORY OF
  JOSIAH HENSON 7

2 THE SLAVE TRADE 18

3 SLAVERY IN THE COLONIES. . . . 34

4 SLAVERY AND REVOLUTION 54

5 KING COTTON 69

6 ABOLITION AND
  EMANCIPATION 85

  TIMELINE 113

  CHAPTER NOTES. 115

  GLOSSARY. 123

  FURTHER READING 124

  INTERNET ADDRESSES
  AND HISTORIC SITES 125

  INDEX 126

American Slavery's Undying Legacy

While the Thirteenth Amendment outlawed slavery in the United States in 1865, the impact of that institution continued to be felt long afterward, and in many ways is still being felt today. The broad variety of experiences encompassed within that epoch of American history can be difficult to encapsulate. Enslaved, free, owner, trader, abolitionist: each "category" hides a complexity of experience as varied as the number of individuals who occupied these identities.

One thing is certain: in spite of how slavery has sometimes been portrayed, very few, if any, enslaved blacks were utter victims who quietly and passively accepted such circumstances. Those who claimed ownership over Africans and African Americans used violence, intimidation, and other means to wield a great degree of power and control. But as human beings—and as laborers within an economic system that depended on labor—all enslaved blacks retained varying degrees of agency within that system.

The "Slavery in American History" series provides a strong and needed overview of the most important aspects of American slavery, from the first transport of African slaves to the American colonies, to the long fight for abolition, to the lasting impact of slavery on America's economy, politics, and culture. Only by understanding American slavery and its complex legacies can we begin to understand the challenge facing not just African Americans, but all Americans: To make certain that our country is a living and breathing embodiment of the principles enunciated in the Constitution of the United States. Only by understanding the past can we mend the present and ensure the rights of our future generations.

—**Henry Louis Gates, Jr.**, *Ph.D., W.E.B. Du Bois Professor of the Humanities, Chair of the Department African and African-American Studies, Director of the W.E.B. Du Bois Institute for African and African-American Research, Harvard University*

Dr. Henry Louis Gates, Jr., Series Advisor

Dr. Henry Louis Gates, Jr., is the author of a number of books including: *The Trials of Phillis Wheatley: America's First Poet and Her Encounters with the Founding Fathers*; *The African-American Century* (with Cornel West); *Little Known Black History Facts*; *Africana: The Encyclopedia of the African American Experience*; *Wonders of the African*

World; *The Future of The Race* (with Cornel West); *Colored People: A Memoir*; *Loose Cannons: Notes on the Culture Wars*; *The Signifying Monkey: Towards A Theory of Afro-American Literary Criticism*; *Figures in Black: Words, Signs, and the Racial Self*; and *Thirteen Ways of Looking at a Black Man*.

Professor Gates earned his M.A. and Ph.D. in English Literature from Clare College at the University of Cambridge. Before beginning his work at Harvard in 1991, he taught at Yale, Cornell, and Duke universities. He has been named one of *Time* magazine's "25 Most Influential Americans," received a National Humanities Medal, and was elected to the American Academy of Arts and Letters.

1

THE STORY OF JOSIAH HENSON

O N JUNE 15, 1789, JOSIAH HENSON WAS BORN a slave in Maryland on a farm near Port Tobacco. His mother was owned by Dr. Josiah McPherson. However, she had been hired out to a second slave owner whose last name was Newman, who owned the nearby farm. Josiah's father was one of Newman's slaves.

Father is Bleeding

Over the years, Josiah's mother worked alongside his father at the Newman farm. Josiah remembered his father as a "good-humored and light-hearted man, the ring-leader in all fun at corn-huskings and Christmas [games.] His banjo was the life of the farm, and . . . at a merry-making would he play on it while the other negroes danced."[1]

Josiah's most vivid memory of his father was his father approaching him with his "head bloody and his back lacerated."[2] At the time, Josiah was only three or four years old. When he was older, he was told the story behind his father's cuts and bruises.

The white slave overseer had lured Josiah's mother away from the field and tried to rape her. As she fought against the overseer's advances, she screamed. Josiah's father heard her cries. He ran toward the sound of her shouts and found her fighting off the overseer. Josiah's father knocked the white overseer down and began beating him. He might have killed his wife's attacker, but Josiah's mother begged her husband to stop. In Maryland, there were laws against a black man hitting a white man. Fearing for his life, the overseer promised not to tell anyone about what Josiah's father had done.

But, once he was out of danger, the overseer did not keep his promise long. Young Josiah's father was found guilty of attacking a white man. He was whipped with one hundred lashes on his bare back, and his right ear was nailed to a post and cut off. After the punishment, Josiah's father became depressed, then defiant, until his owner considered him too disobedient. Josiah's father was "sold South," to another plantation in Alabama. As for Josiah and his mother, they never heard from his father again.

A Leader of Slaves

Just a few years later, when Josiah was five or six, his mother's owner died and the farm's slaves were sold. All five of Josiah's brothers and sisters were sold to different masters and separated from their mother. However, Josiah was sold to the same master as his mother. Josiah was put to work at their new plantation home in Montgomery County, Maryland. He had to carry buckets of water to the slaves working in the fields. As he grew a little older, he hoed weeds among the crop rows. Josiah grew strong from the constant work. He later remembered that by age fifteen, "there were few who could compete with me in work."[3]

By his late teens, Josiah Henson was well-respected by his fellow slaves. His master appointed him superintendent of the farm workers. Henson later said that at age twenty-two, he "married a very efficient, and . . . very well-taught girl, belonging to a neighboring family."[4] Henson was one of the favorites of his master, who continually entrusted him with more responsibility. Through his twenties and into his thirties, Henson oversaw his master's farm. Henson was allowed to leave the plantation and take the farm produce into neighboring towns to sell at market. His master treated him with as much respect as any owner was willing to under slavery.

However, Henson always dreamed of one day

SOURCE DOCUMENT

The overseer called upon the negroes to seize me; but they, knowing something of my physical power, were rather slow to obey. At length they did their best, and as they brought themselves within my reach, I knocked them down successively; and one of them trying to trip up my feet when he was down, I gave him a kick with my heavy shoe, which knocked out several of his front teeth, and sent him groaning away. Meanwhile, the cowardly overseer was availing himself of every opportunity to hit me over the head with his stick, which was not heavy enough to knock me down, though it drew blood freely. At length, tired of the length of the affray, he seized a stake, six or seven feet long, from the fence, and struck at me with his whole strength. In attempting to ward off the blow, my right arm was broken, and I was brought to the ground; where repeated blows broke both my shoulder blades, and made the blood gush from my mouth copiously. The two blacks begged him not to murder me, and he just left me as I was, telling me to learn what it was to strike a white man.[5]

As a slave, Josiah Henson was forced to break up a fight between his master and his master's brother's overseer. The overseer, who was drunk, was knocked to the ground and blamed Henson. A week later, Henson was ambushed while walking through his master's brother's farm while running an errand.

getting his freedom. Loyal to his master, Henson never imagined that he would ever run away. Instead, he planned to one day save enough money to buy his freedom from his master. But saving enough money always proved difficult.

After serving his master for twenty years, Henson was informed one day in the spring of 1825 that his owner was broke. The plantation owner had lost his money in a lawsuit. Henson, his family, and a dozen other slaves were sent off to Kentucky to a large plantation owned by his master's brother. Over the following three years, Henson continued to prove himself a capable supervisor and talented leader of his fellow slaves. He became a minister in the Methodist Episcopal Church. By 1829, after saving several hundred dollars, Henson was prepared to purchase his freedom from his Maryland master. However, he was tricked out of his money by his owner. Soon afterward, his owner started planning to sell Henson south. It was then that Josiah Henson began to consider taking the step he had never given any serious thought: He would escape to freedom.

Traveling at Night, Hiding by Day
Henson believed that he, his wife, and their four children would not be safe even if they escaped to a northern state. He made plans for the six of them to

escape to Canada. However, his wife was not prepared to leave. She feared that they would all be caught while trying to make their way north. After spending an entire night, Josiah still could not convince her. Josiah was so desperate that he told his wife he would leave her and take their three oldest children with him. Finally, she relented and agreed to go with him.

Henson knew that taking his family north would be a difficult task. His youngest children were two and three years old and would have to be carried. Josiah had his wife make a special knapsack with strong straps, which he could throw over his shoulders and carry the two youngsters inside. He even practiced carrying his two children in the large knapsack night after night before their escape. Luckily, Henson's family lived in a cabin near the plantation's river landing. This would allow the family to easily cross the river into the free state of Indiana at night without being seen.

In his role as supervisor, Henson was also sometimes gone for several days, doing business at his owner's farms along the Ohio River. He and his family might be able to get a good head start on their escape before their absence was detected.

By mid-September, Henson and his family were ready to make their secret and dangerous journey. If they were caught, they would be severely punished, and their family might be sold to different owners. On the night of their departure, Henson went up to his master's house and asked to take his oldest son back to his cabin for the night. The family then quietly went down to the river. Among the few goods and food they had packed for their journey, Henson also included a pistol and a knife he had bought illegally from a poor white. At the river, a fellow slave floated them across on a skiff. Henson later wrote: "We were thrown absolutely upon our own poor and small resources, and were to rely on our own strength alone."[6]

Family Provider

For two weeks, Henson and his family moved closer to Canada. They stayed close to a main road, traveling quietly at night and hiding out in nearby woods during the anxious days. Whenever they heard a wagon or buggy approaching at night, they would leave the road and hide until the strangers passed. Bound for the Ohio city of Cincinnati, the family ran out of food two days from the town. The children began to cry with hunger. Henson's wife began to complain to him that they should never have left their plantation life. As for Henson, he was extremely tired from carrying his two children in the special knapsack. He was having trouble sleeping. "My limbs were weary," he later wrote, "and my back and shoulders raw with the burden I

Josiah Henson used his strength and intellect to gain his and his family's freedom.

carried. A fearful dread of detection ever pursued me, and I would start out of my sleep in terror, my heart beating against my ribs, expecting to find the dogs and slave-hunters after me."[7]

Henson took a bold gamble. He left his hungry children alone with his wife in the woods, while he took to the main road in daylight in search of food. At the first house he reached, he was turned away. Fortunately, he came to a second house, where a kind white woman agreed to give him some bread and meat. When Henson tried to pay for the food, she refused.

After giving his family the food, Henson found that his children were soon thirsty. Henson set out again in search of water. He found a small creek, but had nothing in which to carry the water. He tried putting water in his hat, but it leaked out. At last, he hit on a solution. "I took off both shoes, which luckily had no holes in them, rinsed them out, filled them with water, and carried it to my family. They drank it with great delight."[8] Despite the risk of Henson being caught out in the open: "The food . . . put new life and strength into my wife and children when I got back to them again, and we at length arrived safe in Cincinnati."[9]

A Lot of Strife, A Little Help

Once in the Ohio city, the Henson family stayed among some old friends. After a few days of rest, Henson and his family were on the road again. They followed an old military road north and soon found the going slow. The road passed through a thick wilderness region. Here the family's journey became even more difficult. They did not have enough food. Henson was extremely tired from carrying his children. Henson was fearful of an American Indian attack. But still, the family pushed on, with Henson providing them encouragement and a father's leadership.

One afternoon, the Hensons encountered four American Indians along the road. The four American Indians ran away. Fearing the American Indians might return with a party of warriors, Josiah Henson's wife begged him to turn around. But he pushed his family on, telling his wife it was the American Indians who had fled after seeing them, and "it would be a ridiculous thing that both parties should run away."[10]

Henson and his family eventually reached the small

town of Sandusky, near Lake Erie. Hiding his family once again in nearby woods, Josiah approached the lake. He soon spotted a boat tied up to shore. Someone onboard asked Henson if he was looking for work. When Henson said he was, he was put to work loading grain sacks onto the ship. The ship's captain soon realized that Henson was a runaway. The captain proved a friend to Henson and agreed to pick up his family and sail them across the lake to Buffalo, New York, which borders Canada.

Freedom

At Buffalo, with help from the ship's captain, the Hensons were placed on a ferryboat to the Canadian town of Waterloo. They arrived in Canada on October 28, 1830, and Henson immediately began to "throw myself on the ground, and giving way to . . . my feelings, to execute sundry antics which excited the astonishment of those who were looking on."[11] A local man asked what was wrong with Henson. The escaped slave gave a simple response: *I am free.*

Josiah Henson and his family lived in Canada for many years. They found work and lived in a community of blacks, several of whom had also escaped slavery. Henson became a noted minister, learned to read and write, and purchased land of his own. He helped found a school for black students. The black man who had been born into slavery became an advocate of those still held in bondage in the United States. Henson made many trips back to the States, including New York and Massachusetts. His cause became "to aid [other blacks] in every way in my power, and to procure the aid of others for them."[12]

While much of Josiah Henson's story is unique to his experience, there were millions of other blacks, men and women, who endured their own version of slavery. The story of slavery and the history of the United States is a complicated one. It shows deeds inspired by greed and profit, while displaying inspiring examples of struggle, resistance, and survival.

THE SLAVE TRADE

S LAVERY—AN ECONOMIC SYSTEM IN WHICH people own other people as property—is an extremely old institution. People in ancient cultures, living thousands of years ago, kept people as slaves. From Egypt to Sumeria; Babylonia to Assyria; Persia to India; classical Greece to imperial Rome, slavery was a system of labor. While many people today think of slavery as something associated with black Africans, ancient slaves came from any and all races and ethnic groups. By the time of the Middle Ages, a new type of slavery was being created. This system of forced labor was the beginning of black African slavery.[1]

Slavery in the New World

Fifty years before Christopher Columbus discovered the Americas in 1492, Portuguese seamen were cautiously establishing trade connections with African coastal ports. Typically, these Portuguese explorers and traders were seeking such precious items as gold, ivory, and spices. But they soon realized the value and availability of black slaves. In 1441, a Portuguese seaman, Antam Goncalvez, carried two West Africans back to his homeland as a gift to a local prince. This opened the door for a "raid and trade" system of removing Africans from their homelands and shipping them off to labor in communities in Europe or European-controlled islands in the Mediterranean and the eastern Atlantic.[2] During the 1440s, the black slave trade between Africa and Europe took root.

Many of the African slaves the Portuguese brought to Europe were put to work on sugar plantations. By the 1500s, sugar production had become an important part of the economy of Portuguese islands in the Atlantic. Because sugar production required great amounts of labor, the number of African slaves continued to rise.

Beginning with Columbus's first voyage in 1492, Europeans were slowly introduced to the New World, which consisted of North America, South America, and the Caribbean. Sugar production spread to the New World and encouraged the expansion of slavery at an even greater pace. Soon, cane production was one of the most important parts of the European economic system in the Americas. The climate and soil of Brazil

The Portuguese were the first Europeans to start trading goods for African slaves.

proved ideal to sugar production. Later, production developed in the Caribbean.

European Competition for Colonies

The first African slaves were imported to the New World within a decade of Columbus's 1492 voyage to America. By 1600, twenty-five thousand African slaves were working and dying on sugar plantations from Cuba to Hispaniola to Brazil. Such slaves represented a cheap labor force for the Spanish and Portuguese colonizers in the Americas. The labor required of the average African field hand on sugar plantations and in sugar mills was extremely strenuous. Most Africans died only four or five years after their delivery to the New World. Sugar planters had to buy new slaves to replace those who died. But the profits from sugar were so high the slave owners could afford to buy new workers. After all, the owners were not paying the slaves for their work.[3]

For the first century of African slavery in the Americas, the Portuguese controlled much of the human trade system. While the Portuguese had led the way among Europeans, other European powers also became involved in the slave trade. As other Europeans established new colonies in the Americas, slavery soon became part of their economic systems. As early as the 1500s, English traders and shippers were heavily involved in the slave trade. In 1655, the British seized the large island of Jamaica and began organizing their own sugar plantations and mills.

By the 1700s, slaves had become a significant part of English trade. In the seventeenth century, English ships delivered no more than ten thousand slaves during any single decade. But after the turn of the century, the number of English-shipped Africans increased by several times. During the 1730s, for example, Englishmen carried more than forty thousand slaves across the Atlantic to the Americas. The following decade, the number increased by 50 percent. By the 1760s, the figure stood at seventy thousand.

It was only a matter of time until the Caribbean and Brazil were supporting hundreds of thousands of

African slaves. Historians estimate that Europeans shipped 12 million Africans for service in the New World as slaves between 1500 and 1850. Of that number, approximately 2 million died while onboard slave ships somewhere in the Atlantic.[4]

African Origins of Slavery
Putting a face to these millions of enslaved African victims can be difficult. Where in Africa did they come from? How did they become ensnared in the cruel system of slavery? Often they were West Africans, living on or close to the coasts of the modern-day nations of Cape Verde and south to Angola. They came from many different and often warring peoples, perhaps hundreds in all, including Mandingos, Ashantis, Yorubas, Ibos, Sekes, Mbundus, and Bakongos.[5]

The vast majority of these West Africans were farmers or shepherds. They had long ago established elaborate and sophisticated systems of production. They grew rice, fruits, sorghum cane, and millet (a grass eaten by domesticated animals), as well as a wide variety of locally produced roots and vegetables. The West African villagers cleared their lands for farming by burning off the undergrowth of brush. They did not plow their fields, but used digging sticks to plant their crops. Some villagers were also artisans; some were skilled in working with iron.[6]

By the 1500s, the West African cultures included some urban settings. In towns and trade centers, open-air markets and shops offered a wide variety of displayed goods for sale, trade, and barter—including slaves. For centuries prior to the arrival of European traders and shippers along the West African coast, Africans had enslaved one another. But West African slavery practiced before European involvement was different than the later forms. Africans typically enslaved one another only temporarily and rarely for an entire lifetime. Most were captives of wars or simple raiding parties carried out between tribes. Some of those held as slaves were being punished for a crime they had committed. West African traditions and customs often allowed slaves to marry. Children of slaves were not born into slavery, but were considered free.[7]

Before the arrival of Europeans, West Africans had begun conducting trade with outsiders. One trading center was the village outpost of Timbuktu, located along the banks of the upper Niger River. There, local traders bartered with visiting Muslim trade caravans from the East. Part of this trade included the exchange of slaves. So, when trade developed with Europeans after contact along the West African coast, it included buying and selling human beings. These enslaved Africans were then shipped out through the European

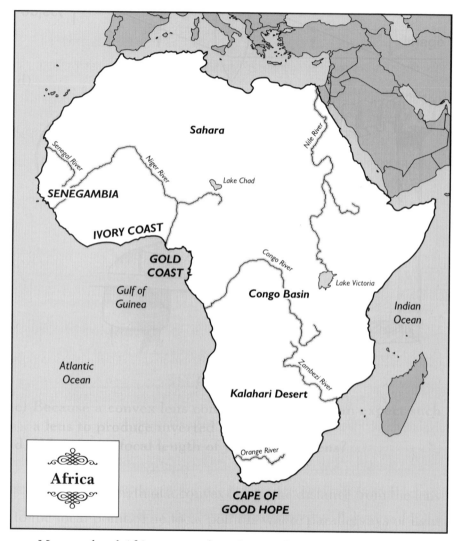

Many enslaved Africans came from Senegambia, the Ivory Coast, or the Gold Coast. Some also came from the interior of Africa.

system of trans-Atlantic trade to Europe and the New World.[8]

Throughout the 1500s, many of the slaves— approximately 40 percent—imported from Africa were picked up in Senegambia (modern-day Senegal) and the West African region of Guinea. During later years, other West African regions were tapped, including the "Gold Coast" (modern-day Ghana), the "Slave Coast" (modern-day Benin), the Ivory Coast, and Nigeria. Slave traders delivered their human exports from the Congo River basin, as well. By 1650, three out of every four slaves were delivered to the coast from Angola and the Congo.[9]

Transatlantic Slavers

To help with the delivery of slaves to the West African coast, the Portuguese established trading posts where slaves and trade goods were bought and sold. The first one constructed was a castle-like fortress called Elmina. Begun in 1481, it was located on the Gold Coast, in the modern-day country of the Republic of Ghana. Although designed to defend the presence of the Portuguese in West Africa, Elmina was also used as a slave-holding facility. Its underground dungeons could hold as many as one thousand slaves.[10] Other similar fortresses were built along the western African coast during the following century by the Portuguese

This view of Elmina fortress also shows European ships in the foreground and an African town to the left of the fortress.

and other European traders and slavers. By 1550, the Dutch, English, French, Danish, Swedish, and Prussians had all built coastal forts for trading slaves. By the early 1700s, there were more than two dozen slave trading posts and forts lined up along more than two hundred miles of the Gold Coast alone.[11]

At these outposts, European buyers viewed the slaves, including people captured on kidnapping raids, called panyarings, into the African interior. Slaves were held in dark prison cells or in vast open pits called barracoons. The prospective purchase, often naked, was examined by merchants and ships' captains. Once a selection was made, the slave was branded on either the back or the buttocks with the merchant's mark. Then, they were taken to the coastal beaches where many of the slaves viewed, for the first time, the Atlantic Ocean.

Many slaves desperately gripped the beach sands, despite receiving lashings from African traders and their hippopotamus-hide whips. Some frightened slaves tried to commit suicide by strangling themselves with their chains. To guard against this, enforcers called "captains of the sand" were posted along the beach to push, beat, prod, and force the slaves into the smaller boats that would carry them out to the immense, white-masted ships that lay off shore. Even as they were transported across the water, some slaves still tried to kill themselves.

How did the Europeans justify the enslavement of millions of Africans? European traders and merchants argued that Africans were better suited for work in the Caribbean than people of other regions. They believed that Africans were able to withstand the heat and humidity of working in the tropics, because such conditions were part of their African experience.

While such a justification was often based in racism, European laborers in the Caribbean did die at a rate much higher than people their same age living in Europe. Africans had natural immunities to tropical diseases that often killed Europeans. However, the work of the slaves in the New World shortened their lives as well.

To ease the consciences of the European buyers in the Caribbean, slave importers often labeled their slaves as "captured in just war." While this was a common trick, most slave buyers in the Americas were careful not to ask about the details of such a claim.

The Middle Passage

Once an African was captured, he or she was brought in chains to the coast where someone bought him or her. Next, the African faced a sea voyage across the Atlantic to the New World. The slaves, many of them speaking languages different from one another, were completely removed from any recognizable surroundings. Many had never even seen a sailing ship. Most of them probably did not understand what lay ahead for them. The voyage across the Atlantic came to be called the Middle Passage. It was the middle leg of a variety of trade "triangles" that often included a voyage from England to Africa, Africa to the New World, and the New World back to England.

Slave ships were vessels used to transport as much human cargo as possible to increase the profits of each voyage. There was no intent to create any comfort for the Africans themselves. The levels below the upper deck usually measured six feet in length and less than three feet in height.

Slaves had to lie down in cramped quarters, packed together. Many slavers jammed the slaves together, allowing no more than eighteen inches of space (lying down) for each captive, providing, as one observer noted, as "much room as a man in his coffin."[12] Another observer described how "400 wretched beings [were] crammed into a [ship's] hold 12 yards in length . . . and only 3 1/2 feet in height."[13] Onboard one crowded ship, the slaves experienced the heat in the ship's hold and panicked, desperate for fresh air. Fifty-four slaves were crushed to death as a result.

Some slavers believed that overcrowding on slave ships was not the best means of delivering enslaved Africans. They thought that additional space for each slave resulted in a greater rate of survival, giving profits a boost. But most slave ship captains forced their slaves to live with a minimum of space. Often a ship loaded more slaves than it was designed to hold. One ship, built to carry 450 slaves, was more typically packed with 600 people below decks. Slave ship captains gained reputations based on whether they were "tight packers" or "loose packers."[14]

Below decks, there was no consideration for sanitation, causing the hold of the vessel to reek with a sickening odor. The slaves were chained together in long rows, with the irons attached to their ankles. They generally had to lie on hard wooden planks because there was not enough room to stand up completely.

Life was often the same series of events from day to day. Each morning, the ship's crew opened up the hold and ordered groups of Africans to come up on deck. There, they received a breakfast of beans. Slaves were typically fed twice daily. The food might consist of boiled rice, millet, or cornmeal. Small amounts of salted beef might be mixed in. A common food was

Africans faced crowded, unsanitary conditions on slave ships.

called "horse beans." The beans were boiled to a gloppy consistency and mixed with palm oil and red pepper. Other foods included stewed yams, manioc (a starchy root also known as cassava), and plantains (a bananalike plant). Many slavers required their human cargo to carry out a ritual known as "dancing the slave." As one slave provided the beat by pounding on an iron kettle or perhaps an African musical instrument similar to a banjo, called a "banjar," the slaves leaped about the deck in a bizarre fashion. The purpose of the ritual was to give them exercise. Slaves were kept on deck to receive the benefits of fresh air and sunshine. But, come nightfall, they were sent below to spend another dreaded night of crowded existence.[15]

Ship crews later remembered the sounds of the hundreds of slaves below: crying men, women, and children; the moans of the sick; and the wails of the dying. Their circumstances led some slaves to attempt suicide by refusing to eat. They were often force-fed by having food jammed down their throats through a funnel called a "speculum oris." Some slaves jumped overboard. So many slaves attempted suicide by this method that it was reported that sharks sometimes followed slave ships across the Atlantic.[16]

Reaching the New World

When a slave ship arrived in a Caribbean port, it would generally cause lots of excitement. A typical port was dominated by a savanna, or central market square, where the islanders sold their goods, produce, and other handmade wares. Such ports often included locals called factors—men who were employed by sugar plantation owners to buy slaves as they arrived from Africa. Sometimes the plantation owner himself might make a trip to the port to buy his own slaves.[17]

Slaves were sold according to their potential value, beginning with those who were considered of less worth. These included the sick, the disfigured, and those who had been severely injured by beatings. Some had lost a limb, a foot, or a hand due to some punishment they received. These slaves—called "refuse"—did not bring high prices. They were brought ashore and put up for bid at a public auction. This seaside bargaining was held "by inch of candle." The bidding for each damaged person lasted until a candle had burned one inch. At that time, the bidding was ended and the highest bids took ownership. Those slaves who were not purchased because of their low value were no longer held. They had become useless property and were soon released to fend for themselves in a strange land. Usually such Africans died from neglect and starvation.[18]

For those slaves who were healthy, robust, and assumed to make good field hands, their sale took place during a "scramble." This time, however, there would be no bidding. The buying would take place onboard the slaver to minimize the possibility of a valuable African running away. The ship's captain set a price for each slave beforehand and made each amount known to the potential buyers. After a signal, the buyers would dash toward these highly prized slaves. Each would take possession of a slave he wanted to purchase. Once the deal was struck, the interested planters took the Africans to their plantations to begin their lives of perpetual slavery.[19]

SLAVERY IN THE COLONIES

THE COLONIAL SLAVE TRADE BECAME A FRENZY of competition. Portuguese ships delivered most of the Africans to the New World, especially to Brazil. Black slaves were imported in greater numbers after Central and South American Indian laborers proved inadequate. Within fifty years of Columbus's first voyage to the Western Hemisphere, the Spanish were importing ten thousand African workers to the Americas each year.[1]

Yet, by the seventeenth century, the Spanish empire was in decline, having faced extensive challenge from the English. As early as the 1620s, the English were in control of slave markets on the island of St. Christopher, Barbados, and by the 1630s were trading in Antigua and Montserrat. Jamaica, one of the largest slave-trading islands of the Caribbean, fell into the hands of the English by 1655. By the 1640s, the Dutch

West India Company had established extensive slave trade links with their own island markets in Curaçao, St. Eustatius, and Tobago. The French Company of the Islands of America was active on the islands of Guadeloupe, Martinique, and Marie Galante. The lucrative slave trade of the New World had become, by the 1600s, a common extension of European economies.[2]

Sugar Plantations

Because the great profits in the Caribbean rested on sugar production, the vast majority of those Africans imported into the region were forced to work on sugar plantations. The average sugar plantation in the Caribbean included several hundred acres of culti-vated cane fields, while some larger plantations might include as many as one thousand acres. The largest plantations might work hundreds of slaves and pro-duce nearly one hundred tons of sugar annually.

One of the most prosperous sugar planters in the seventeenth century Caribbean was an Englishman named Henry Drax. His cane fields spanned more than seven hundred acres on the island of Barbados. He held more than three hundred African slaves and oper-ated two sugar mills. Not only did he produce sugar, but he siphoned off molasses, as well, and operated a distillery, which turned the molasses into rum. In

1680, his plantation and mill operations allowed him to export five thousand pounds of sugar, molasses, and rum. Three years later, he and his island contemporaries shipped twenty thousand tons of sugar back to England. One year's sugar and molasses exports kept three hundred ships busy in the Atlantic.[3] Such involved and lucrative operations guaranteed the constant need for greater importation of African slaves. The majority of the black slaves brought to the New World onboard English slave ships were sold for labor on sugar plantations.[4]

Slave Life on the Islands

Although each island slave's experience was unique, many shared common circumstances. Working on a sugar plantation meant long days of ten to twelve hours

Once it was harvested, sugar cane was often processed into molasses, which was then made into rum. Slaves did most of the work throughout the whole process.

of hard labor. When the sugar cane was ready to harvest, the workday was often extended to as long as eighteen hours. The workers were provided with one half-hour rest period for breakfast and a two-hour break during the hottest part of the afternoon. Those who worked the sugar cane fields under the hot island sun included men, women, and even children. Field hands were watched over by a "jumper," a white worker who was skilled in the use of a whip. Slaves were often worked to death. Because sugar production generated such high profits for the plantation owners, slaves were considered expendable, and easily replaced.[5] During some years, slave deaths exceeded slave births. On the island of St. Vincent, for example, during one year, 2,656 blacks were born while African slave deaths exceeded 4,200.[6]

For those slaves who tried to escape, the punishments were severe. Those who organized runaways were usually hanged. For those who ran away and were later recovered, a common punishment was to have one leg chopped off if the slave had been gone for as long as three months. If the escaped slave had been gone for as long as six months, the punishment was usually death. If a slave tried to kill his or her master, he or she was stretched across a wagon wheel and tied to it. Then, each of the slave's bones was broken with a crowbar. Even a slave who hit a white person was dealt with sharply, having his right hand cut off.[7]

The numbers tell the story of the increasing reliance European colonizers in the New World had on Africans for their primary work force. On the island of Barbados, for example, by 1640, only a few hundred black slaves had been imported. Once sugar plantations were established and proved profitable, the number had increased to six thousand by 1645. Just five years later, the number had increased to twenty thousand. By 1700, the black slave population of Barbados had risen to eighty thousand.[8]

Such slaves were typically provided two meals daily, which often included cornmeal, salted pork, fish, and beans. Most foods were not produced on the islands, because plantation owners wanted to plant as much of their lands in sugar as possible. Some slaves produced supplemental foods for themselves on small plots, which they farmed on Sundays or holidays. As for their other daily necessities, island slaves were provided with few clothes. Often they received their clothing allotment once a year, consisting of pants and shirts for the men, while women received simple calico dresses. Children often went naked until they reached the age of four or five.[9] Slave houses were small and poorly built, and included few pieces of furniture. A bed might be no more than a cloth mattress filled with cornhusks.

Slaves and the British Colonies

The high profits generated by sugar production led to the dramatic expansion of African slavery during the 1600s. But black slavery was slow to develop in what was to become the United States. In 1607, an English joint stock company, the Virginia Company of London, established a settlement along the banks of a river that they named after their King James I. The colony proved to be the first permanent English colony in North America.

It was here, at Jamestown, that the first black workers were introduced to the British colony of Virginia in 1619. Jamestown colony resident John Rolfe describes the introduction of these first black workers to the British colony: "About the last of August came a dutch man of warre that sold us twenty Negars."[10] The *Jesus of Lubeck, a* dutch ship, had delivered these Africans into North America for the sole purpose of providing labor. Historians have not been able to agree whether they were indentured servants (required to work for a limited number of years only) or slaves. Virginia was not a sugar-producing colony. It did, however, rely on tobacco production. (Rolfe had introduced a mild variety of Caribbean tobacco for cultivation in Virginia in 1611.) With the import of these twenty African workers, the seeds of North American slavery were being planted.[11]

The first American effort at slave importation proved a dismal failure. In 1645, a Boston ship, the *Rainbow,* sailed to the Guinea Coast, where the ship's captain found few slaves available at the trading posts. In time, the impatient ship's captain led a slave-catching expedition and went into the interior. The effort resulted in the capture of only two slaves. When the *Rainbow* returned to Boston, the captain ran into trouble when it was revealed that his slave-catching raid had occurred on a Sunday, outraging the local Puritan population. The captain was arrested and soon stood trial for murder, man-stealing, and breaking the Sabbath (working on a Sunday). He was only acquitted when the Massachusetts Bay court elders realized they had no authority over a man's actions outside of their colony. The two slave captives were released and returned to their African homes.[12]

Although African workers were introduced into the British colony of Virginia by 1619, those workers may not have been considered as slaves, owned by masters and bound to work for their entire lives. It appears that, for the most part, many of the first black workers introduced in the Tidewater region of Virginia and its neighbor colony just to the north, Maryland, were treated and defined no differently than white workers. Blacks listed in the Virginia census for 1623 and 1624 were not referred to as "slaves" but as "servants," just as whites were. The number of blacks imported to the British colonies of North America remained low for most of the seventeenth century. There was plenty of labor, because many of those whites migrating to the colonies became indentured servants. Such workers typically served a master for five to seven years, then were free to make their own way. Many such workers became indentured servants to pay their ship passage to the New World. Even thirty years after the first twenty blacks were introduced at the Jamestown colony, Virginia had no more than three hundred black workers out of a population of more than fifteen thousand inhabitants, not including American Indians. By 1640, the institution of black slavery was beginning to develop. However, it would take a generation or two to create a fully formed slave system in British North America.[13]

Developing a System of Slavery

As late as 1661, there were no laws in Virginia recognizing slavery. However, many of the black people brought to Virginia by that time were no longer identified the same as white workers. Contracts of the time referred to such black workers as "servants for life" or as "perpetual servants."[14] During the 1660s, then, new laws in Virginia began to lay out a legally recognized system of black slavery. By 1705, all such laws in Virginia were codified into a complete system. Called the Virginia Negro Codes, these laws limited and controlled the movement and freedoms of Virginia slaves. Under such laws, slaves could not testify in court against any white person, could not own property, and were restricted from freely assembling together. All slaves had to carry passes when traveling away from their masters' estates. Slaves' marriages were not legally recognized.[15]

What caused landowners in Virginia to move away from using indentured servants and establish a slave labor force? There are several reasons. During the first half of the seventeenth century, it was cheaper to rely on indentured servants than purchase slaves. This was due to the high death rate among both white and black workers who reached the Americas. During an immigrant's first five years in the colonies, he or she had a 50 percent chance of dying. Because a slave cost double that of an indentured servant, it was not worth it to purchase slaves. Indentured servants were the better deal. There were also plenty of white indentured servants available. But by the 1660s, the number of indentured servants coming to America had dropped significantly due to better living circumstances in Great Britain. With fewer indentured workers available, employers turned to slavery. In cooperation, the Virginia colonial legislature, the House of Burgesses, began creating a legal system allowing slavery.[16]

Other British colonies in North America followed suit. New York institutionalized slavery for life in 1665.[17] By 1671, Maryland began passing laws defining and establishing black slavery within its borders. Soon, slavery was a legal system of labor in the British colonies, both north and south.[18] After the legalization of slavery in the British colonies, the number of black workers in the colonies soon dramatically increased. In 1680, for example, the number of white servants in Maryland was four times the number of slaves. But by 1710, slaves outnumbered white servants five to one.[19] By 1700, nearly one of every three non-American Indian residents of South Carolina was a black. Due to the demand on their labor, just a decade later, Africans outnumbered whites.

Several factors allowed the expansion and development of slavery in the British colonies of North America. One of the most significant was the granting of the *asiento*—special permission granted by the Spanish crown to import slaves to the New World. During the sixteenth century, the Catholic Church forbid Spain from engaging in the slave trade. The

SOURCE DOCUMENT

. . . for the first offence of hog stealing commited by a negro or slave he shall be carried before a justice of the peace of the county where the fact was commited before whome being convicted of the said offence by one evidence or by his owne confession he shall . . . receive on his bare back thirty nine lashes well laid on, and for the second offence such negro or slave upon conviction before a court of record shall stand two hours in the pillory and have both his eares nailed thereto and at the expiration of the said two hours have his ears cutt off close by the nailes . . .[20]

This 1699 Virginia law became part of the slave codes. It lays out the punishment for slaves or any other blacks who stole hogs.

Spanish colonies in the New World needed slaves, so the Spanish monarchs granted the monopoly, or *asiento*, to the highest bidder among other countries. In 1713, after the British emerged victorious in the War of the Spanish Succession, they won the right of *asiento*. This allowed England to import many slaves into its American colonies to provide labor across the South.[21]

The Triangular Trade

Although the number of slaves in the North, especially the New England colonies, was never very significant, the region was heavily involved in the slave trade by the 1700s. New Englanders decided to build distilleries where Caribbean-produced molasses could be processed into rum. Large barrels, called hogsheads, filled with rum could then be transported across the Atlantic onboard New England ships, where it could then be traded for slaves. New England "Yankee" merchants and shippers could exchange approximately one hundred gallons of rum, with a value of fifty dollars, for a black slave. The New Englanders would then transport the slaves to the West Indies. The trade yielded high profits, because each slave could be sold for three to four times what the American sea captains had purchased him or her for in Africa. They then picked up fresh quantities of molasses which would be processed in New England distilleries into rum and the entire process would begin all over again. This trade—connecting New England, Africa, and the Caribbean—became known as the Triangular Trade.[22]

During the eighteenth century, New England shippers could make their fortunes trading across the Atlantic, bringing slaves from Africa to the Caribbean. Just a single voyage could result in great profits. Through one such voyage, which included taking

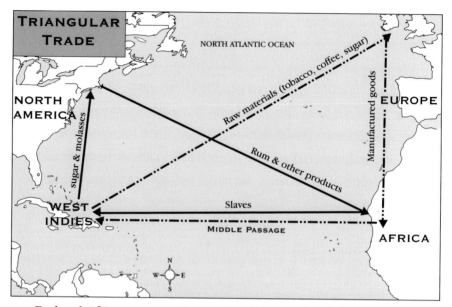

Enslaved Africans were subject to the vicious cycle of the Triangular Trade, which included the Middle Passage.

slaves across the Middle Passage, two American traders from Newport, Rhode Island, earned a profit of over thirteen hundred pounds. This was equal to more than ten years of wages for an average worker of the day. While profits were typically high, such shipping involved many risks and failure was always possible. Dozens of traders, ship captains, and New England merchants began to profit from the slave trade. Newport, in fact, was one of the most popular ports for the Triangular Trade. During the colonial period, Newport alone was home to between forty and fifty slave ships. The coastal town was home to twenty-two distilleries (as well as three sugar refineries), which produced much of the rum that was traded in exchange for African slaves. By 1763, there were sixty-three distilleries near two additional New England centers, Boston and Salem. These rum factories used 15,000 hogsheads of molasses to produce 12,500 hogsheads of rum annually. The profits from rum were often tremendous.[23]

Southern Agriculture and Slavery

In the South, the number of slaves had grown to great numbers by the early eighteenth century. There, a slave culture developed. While tobacco was grown in the Lower South, as well, slaves often worked the rice fields where that grain crop had become extremely popular by 1715. By the mid-1700s, the British colonial south was actually two regions: the Chesapeake or Tidewater South and the Lower South. The oldest southern colonies were those of the Chesapeake, which included Virginia and Maryland. The Lower South colonies were the Carolinas and Georgia.

The South of the 1700s was a region dominated by three racial groups. Whites were the first group. The second group was the blacks, the majority of whom were slaves. American Indians were the last group. They consisted of the original inhabitants of the

Atlantic Coastal region that still lived on the fringes of European colonial society. They traded with whites just as their ancestors had in the early 1600s. Of the racial groups living in the South, black slaves constituted 40 percent of the region's population by 1750.

Developing Slave Culture

In some portions of the South, the plantations were the most significant social and economic institution. By 1750, a typical southern plantation featured a large house, often set on a high place, dominating the surrounding fields and farmlands. Slaves often referred to such a home as "the Big House." Outbuildings might

During the eighteenth century, one of the main crops in the South was rice, to which slaves often tended. These slaves are hoeing weeds that have grown near the rice plants.

include a smokehouse, summer kitchen, barns, stables, corn cribs, and drying sheds for tobacco. Slaves lived in primitive wooden cabins with dirt floors. Such shacks were cold in the winter and hot in the summer. Several families might occupy the same small cabin.

The world created by the slaves in the British colonies became, over time, a mixture of both African elements and those they discovered in their new-world homes. One element of their African existence, which did not survive for the most part, was their native languages. Because slaves from different tribal origins were purchased and worked on the same plantations and farms, the black workers spoke different languages from one another. Their owners were European, so the slaves began to lose their African languages. Some dialects, as well as several African words, did survive. The Gullah and Geechee dialects, found on the Sea Islands of South Carolina and Georgia, as well as in the coastal cities of Charleston and Savannah, can still be found today. They have combined English language structures with African words, creating a creolized, or mixed, language. Other African influences on English-produced words are still in use: yam, banjo, tote, goober (for "peanut"), cooter (tortoise), gumbo, ananse (spider), samba, tabby (a type of building material), and voodoo.[24]

Another aspect of West African life that blacks

A planter's mansion was huge in comparison to the slaves' tiny quarters (right).

brought to the New World and adapted in their new environs was music. Many black slaves sang while working the fields in America, as well as during religious activities. Some forms of African singing, such as the call-and-response style (known as "antiphonal singing"), had been common in Africa and remained so among displaced black slaves. Drums and horns had been important African instruments. However, many slave owners did not allow their slaves to use them, believing that their slaves used them to communicate with one another. But another African instrument, the *mbanza*, did survive the black slave experience. The *mbanza* consisted of a gourd with a wooden neck attached to it and strings made from animal gut. In America, the instrument led to the development of the banjo. Slaves also used instruments they were introduced to in the British colonies, such as the fiddle and the guitar. African music would continue to affect black American music for many generations.[25]

Slave Resistance and Rebellion

Most, if not all, slaves did not give in to miserable lives of degrading treatment. The slave system was often based on intimidation and the threat of punishment. Women were sometimes mistreated sexually. For many, they faced the threat of brutal punishments if they did not work and generally cooperate with their white owners. Unwilling to accept such treatment for life, slaves resisted, choosing to run off from their owners, nonviolently resist their owners, or, more dramatically, to rebel outright.

When Africans first arrived at their New World destinations, they could be defiant, slow to work, and generally uncooperative. One master noted: "You would really be surpris'd at their Perseverance. They often die before they can be conquered."[26] During the early years of the thirteen colonies, when settlements were scattered thinly, slaves might escape, usually with those who spoke their language, hiding out in the forests and nearby river bottoms. These escapees were called "outliers." They often raided and stole from white farms and plantations, including those of their former masters, to stay alive. By the late 1600s, some southern colonies, including Virginia and South Carolina, offered bounties to anyone who killed an "outlier."[27]

Slaves also refused to cooperate with their masters in less obvious ways than running away. Some slaves did not work as fast as they could, holding their productivity to a minimum. Others secretly destroyed their master's equipment, tools, even the crops in the field. Such activities were often noticed by slave owners, causing them to have a poor opinion of their black workers.

The form of resistance whites feared most was the open slave rebellion or revolt. Such actions taken by slaves often resulted in the deaths of both whites and blacks. Slave revolts were rare compared to the instances of quiet resistance or escape. However, two waves of rebellion saw several slave revolts, including the years 1710–1722 and 1730–1740. The two most notable slave revolts in the thirteen colonies occurred in New York in 1712 and in South Carolina in 1739.

The 1712 revolt involved twenty-seven slaves who rebelled against the harsh treatment they were receiving by burning a building and seizing arms. These slave rebels killed nine white men and wounded another six, using firearms, swords, and hatchets. The revolt was halted by a local militia unit. Of the twenty-seven black rebels, six committed suicide and the remaining twenty-one were executed.

The September 1739 revolt, known as the Stono Rebellion, took place twenty miles outside Charleston near Stone Bridge. A slave named Jemmy or Tommy, who had only recently come from Angola, led a group of slaves to a "wearehouse, & then plundered it of guns & ammunition." Several white men were killed. As the escapees moved toward Spanish Florida, more slaves joined them until they numbered approximately one hundred. They attacked plantations and killed several dozen people. A group of planters and local American Indians, riding on horseback, caught up with the escaped slaves and killed forty-four of them, while the others escaped capture.[28]

The institution of slavery became firmly established, and the southern way of life often featured slave labor at its center. Slavery appeared to be a permanent way of life for countless thousands of blacks. But as many colonists began to reconsider their relationship with Great Britain and political revolution appeared on the horizon, some slaves became hopeful that the newly raised voices calling for liberty and independence might change their lives as well.

CHAPTER 4

SLAVERY AND
REVOLUTION

BY 1750, SLAVERY WAS A SIGNIFICANT PART OF the economies of all the British colonies, especially in the south. Everywhere—from the Maryland Tidewater to Georgia—slavery was a basic source of labor. The institution was well defined by British and colonial law. But slavery was less important in the northern colonies. Of the entire slave population in the thirteen British colonies of North America, 90 percent of slaves lived in the South. In South Carolina, the black population had grown larger than the number of whites. In 1740, 25 percent of the non-American Indian residents of the southern colonies were black slaves. Over the following thirty years, black slaves came to represent 40 percent of the southern population.[1]

As for the northern colonies, the number of slaves was significantly fewer. Of the nearly seven hundred thousand slaves in the thirteen colonies, the Middle colonies—New York, Pennsylvania, New Jersey, and Delaware—were home to only thirty-six thousand slaves. New England had a slave population of fewer than four thousand. By far, the vast majority of black slaves in the North American colonies were held by southern colonies—nearly 660,000.[2]

Slaves were imported into the British colonies during every decade of the eighteenth century. Eighty thousand Africans were imported to Virginia and Maryland between 1700 and 1770. But a greater number developed because slave couples were having children. In fact, the British colonies of North America were the first in the Americas to develop slave populations that grew without constant additional imports of fresh slaves to the colonies. Natural increase could occur in the North American colonies because slaves were never considered expendable, as they were in the Caribbean islands or in South America. This fact is an important one. The colonies that later became the early United States represent the only place in the New World where the black slave population was able to sustain itself and even increase its own numbers naturally. By comparison, from 1681 through 1791, the French imported 860,000 black slaves to its sugar island of Saint-Domingue. Yet, by 1791, the number of slaves there was only 480,000. By the 1770s, the majority of slaves in America had been born in the colonies.[3]

Just how many black people were forcibly imported into North America is not exactly known. However, the records of such things as slave ships, bills of sale, and tax records in various New World ports indicate the general number. By 1790, approximately 275,000 blacks had been imported into the British colonies and subsequently the United States. During the following two decades (the slave trade to America was banned by Congress in 1808) perhaps another seventy thousand were imported to the United States. Illegal slave trading may have introduced another fifty thousand during the fifty years leading up to the Civil War (1861–1865). An additional twenty-eight thousand were imported to North America by the Spanish and French through New Orleans while the port was under their control. When these figures are added together, approximately 425,000 slaves reached North America throughout a period of nearly 250 years. This figure equals less than 5 percent of the total number of African slaves who were imported into the New World, beginning in the early 1500s.[4]

The Approaching Revolution

By the 1760s and 1770s, slavery was an important extension of British colonial life. But during those decades, many colonists moved into open rebellion against the British Crown. Both King George III and Parliament pushed new taxes and other controls on colonial trade and commerce, which the colonists considered oppressive. In 1775, British Redcoats and Massachusetts colonial militiamen fired on one another in April in the towns of Lexington and Concord. The American Revolution had begun, and it offered colonists a new filter for viewing the slavery they had come to rely on.

The word on the lips of every American patriot by 1776 was "liberty." Colonials wanted to be free of British control. As freedom and liberty became common goals for many patriots, the institution of slavery began to appear different to some of them. To some, both southerners and northerners, it made little sense to talk seriously of ending British oppression while maintaining the ownership of blacks as slaves. As one Massachusetts patriot leader, James Otis, observed: "The Colonists are by law of Nature free born as indeed all men are, white or black. . . . Does it follow that 'tis right to enslave a man because he is black?"[5] When in 1776 the fiery rebel writer, Thomas Paine, penned his popular pamphlet, *Common Sense*, which supported the concept of independence from Great Britain, he noted how patriots sometimes "complain so loudly of attempts to enslave them," yet those same men are slave owners who "hold so many hundred thousands in slavery; and annually enslave many thousands more."[6] Yet another revolutionary leader, Benjamin Rush, tried to convince his fellow colonists the "the plant of liberty is of so tender a nature, that it cannot thrive long in the neighborhood of slavery."[7]

Blacks and the Revolution

During the demonstrations against the hated British Stamp Act, blacks in Boston participated in the protests. When a Boston mob broke into riot against a local garrison of British troops in March 1770, blacks participated. Future president John Adams, who defended the British soldiers in court, later described the street protest as including "saucy boys, Negroes and mulattoes, Irish teagues and outlandish jacktars [sailors]."[8] The riot resulted in the British soldiers firing their muskets into the crowd, killing five Bostonians, including a twenty-seven-year-old free black named Crispus Attucks. When the shots were fired at Lexington and Concord, signaling the arrival of the Revolutionary War, Massachusetts militia troops, known as Minutemen, included blacks in their ranks.

In the north, slaves took special advantage of the

This nineteenth century lithograph by John Bufford depicts the death of Crispus Attucks at the Boston Massacre.

era's revolutionary spirit. Slaves petitioned colonial governments for their freedom and called for an end to slavery. In the spring of 1773, one group of slaves from Boston presented a petition to the Massachusetts General Court in the town of Thompson, calling for their freedom. The Massachusetts assemblymen had sought their own freedom from the rule of Great Britain; therefore, the small group of four slaves expected the Massachusetts leaders to free them from slavery. The petition stated that the slaves expected "great things from men who have made such a noble stand against the designs of their *fellow-men* to enslave them." The slaves who appealed for their freedom, in the same petition, also stated their desire to return to Africa in the future.[9] Some slaves took their masters to court and sued for their freedom. In Massachusetts, Caesar Hendrick claimed his master had denied him his natural right to be free. An all-white jury agreed. Hendrick won his case and was freed. But such cases were rare.

Slaves and the Revolutionary Ideal
Despite the hopes of many blacks that the American Revolution might lead to an end to American slavery, the institution did not come crashing down. The patriot leader Thomas Jefferson penned the *Declaration of Independence* in the hot summer of 1776, stating that "all men are created equal; that they are endowed by their Creator with certain unalienable rights; that among these are life, liberty, and the pursuit of happiness." Yet even as he wrote those words founded in the ideas of freedom, he did not mean them to apply to slaves—or to black people in general. Such patriot leaders as Jefferson and Washington, in fact, were slave owners.

However, blacks fought in the American Revolutionary War. Many hoped that by taking sides they could help bring about their own freedom. They found reasons to support either the patriots or the

Here, George Washington and his stepchildren are seen in a field with his slaves. The slaves in this painting are dressed in much nicer clothes than those which were usually provided in real life.

British. Some British authorities promised to free any and all slaves who escaped into the hands of British. As a result, tens of thousands of slaves escaped behind British lines. A small number of them joined and fought with British forces, including Americans loyal to the king (called Loyalists). Many of those slaves who joined the British left the new United States after the patriots won the American Revolution. Thousands of runaway slaves were taken by Loyalists to Florida, the Caribbean, and to Nova Scotia in Canada.

Approximately five thousand slaves fought alongside American forces during the Revolutionary War and participated in battles from Lexington and Concord to the last great field engagement at Yorktown, in October 1781.[10] For his service in the battles of Lexington and Concord, one black slave, Peter Salem, was granted his freedom. Another, Salem Poor, was given a commendation for his bravery during the battle of Bunker Hill in the summer of 1775. Poor later served under Washington and was part of the army that wintered at Valley Forge in 1777–1778.[11]

Blacks in Uniform

Blacks were not easily accepted, however, into the ranks of the revolutionary Continental Army. In the

Peter Salem was also at the Battle of Bunker Hill and shot and killed British Major John Pitcairn.

spring and summer of 1775, General George Washington issued orders opposing the enlistment of any new black troops and even the reenlistment of those already in the Continental Army. Many whites, including Washington, did not think black men were capable of fighting, considering them to be too fearful to fight well in the heat of battle. However, in early November, the royal governor of Virginia, Lord Dunmore, offered slaves their freedom in exchange for becoming part of "His Majesty's Troops . . . for the more speedily reducing this Colony to the proper sense of their duty to His Majesty's crown and dignity." The call from Dunmore was answered by three hundred black slaves who escaped and joined the British ranks within a week of the proclamation.[12]

In all, approximately eight hundred slaves fled their masters to take up arms with the British who offered them freedom. Few of them saw any fighting, however. Dunmore organized them into a special black regiment called "Lord Dunmore's Ethiopian Regiment." But violent outbreaks of smallpox onboard British warships ravaged their numbers, killing as many as five hundred.[13]

Washington soon changed his mind about keeping blacks out of American uniforms. The month after Dunmore's regiment was organized, General Washington noted: "If that man, Dunmore, is not crushed before the Spring he will become the most dangerous man in America. His strength will increase like a snowball running down hill. Success will depend on which side can arm the Negro faster." By December 30, 1775, Washington opened the ranks of the Continental Army to black soldiers.[14]

SOURCE DOCUMENT

That it is suggested . . . that a force might be raised in the said State from among the negroes which would not only be formidable to the enemy from their numbers and the discipline . . . but would also lessen the danger from revolts and desertions by detaching the most vigorous and enterprizing from among the negroes. . . .

Resolved, That it be recommended to . . . South Carolina and Georgia, to consider of the Necessity, and Utility of arming [and] raising a force of able bodied Negroes . . .[15]

The above passage was in the journal entry of the Continental Congress for Monday, March 29, 1779. The congress had decided to enlist slaves in the fight against the British. (Note: Up until the twentieth century, African Americans were often called Negroes. Today, however this term is often considered hurtful and impolite.)

Opening the Continental Army's ranks to black troops began to have an impact on the American military and the institution of slavery in a short time. Within a year, troop shortages caused the Continental Congress and several state governments to call for the recruitment of blacks in greater numbers. By 1777, entire regiments of black troops were being formed in Rhode Island. That same year, neighboring Connecticut allowed masters to free their slaves to serve in the state militia or the Continental Army. Other states, including New York and New Jersey, also followed that example. Few southern states passed such laws. Only Maryland allowed slaves their freedom in exchange for their military service. Several other southern states—including Virginia and North Carolina—allowed slaves to take the place of their masters in the state militia. This practice frequently led to such slaves being freed. Some slaves, after fighting in the army and gaining their freedom, renamed themselves, taking new last names such as Jeffery *Liberty* and Ned *Freedom*.[16] Blacks became commonplace in the ranks of the Continental Army.[17]

So many blacks served willingly alongside American patriots that the revolution caused several state legislatures, especially in New England, to at least consider freeing all the slaves in their states. Even before the end of the war, the abolition of slavery was a recurring topic of debate and discussion. Blacks filed petitions in several New England states, calling for the end of slavery. A significant movement among whites was soon underway to abolish slavery completely from the new United States. Among whites, the religious group known as the Quakers, or the Society of Friends, led the way. As a religious body, Quakers were opposed to slavery, calling for equality and brotherhood between the races. Quakers formed antislavery societies. Even before the opening of the Revolutionary War, the Quakers were joining vocal blacks in calling for an end to slavery.[18]

End of Northern Slavery

The result of such considerable pressure was an end to northern slavery. By 1784, every northern state—with the exception of New Jersey and New York—had passed legislation either calling for the immediate end of slavery or a plan of gradual emancipation of slaves. In Virginia, the new state legislature required the freeing of any slaves who had fought alongside patriot troops during the Revolutionary War. One slave owner in Maryland, Philip Graham, chose to free all his slaves, having become convinced that "fellow men in bondage and slavery is repugnant to the gold law of God and the unalienable right of mankind as well as to every principle of the late glorious revolution which has taken place in America."[19] Even in the Deep South, where the slave culture was most deeply engrained, new laws were passed calling for an end to the abusive excesses of slavery.

Economic changes in the Tidewater region of Virginia and Maryland also had a dramatic impact on the nature and extent of slavery practiced there. The Revolutionary War had brought about a drop in the production of tobacco in those new states. As planters saw a drop in the price of tobacco, they shifted their fields to grain production, instead, raising wheat and corn. These crops required less intensive labor and fewer full-time slave laborers. In some cases, slave owners allowed at least some of their slaves freedom after a number of years of service, rather than holding them for life. This dramatically increased the number of free blacks in such states. In Virginia, for example, the number of free blacks in 1782 was fewer than two thousand. By 1790, that number had risen to nearly thirteen thousand and, by 1810, was greater than thirty thousand.[20]

While the southern states did not lay a course for the elimination of slavery within their borders after the American Revolution, they did reluctantly join ranks with the northern states in limiting the expansion of slavery. The Constitutional Convention was held in the summer of 1787 in Philadelphia. After much debate, the states agreed on a date for closing the international slave trade to the United States. The states agreed to ban any new imports of slaves into their borders after 1808. Also, during the 1780s, the Congress under the Articles of Confederation organized a portion of the territory the United States had gained from Great Britain following the American Revolution. The Old Northwest Territory—the modern-day states of Ohio, Indiana, Illinois, Michigan, and Wisconsin—was established, under the Ordinance of 1787, without slavery.

By the end of the 1780s, a serious change was in the wind concerning the future of slavery in America. There appeared to be progress toward ending the institution. Laws allowing owners to free their slaves, called manumission laws, were loosened, making it easier for a slave owner to free his or her slaves. Under new state laws, slaves were able to purchase their own freedom in Virginia (1782), Delaware (1787), Maryland (1790), and the new state of Kentucky (1792). Yet even as events presented possibilities for the ultimate demise of American slavery, the institution would survive.

5

KING COTTON

I N THE YEARS DURING AND FOLLOWING THE
American Revolution, the southern agriculture
system experienced dramatic change. Warfare during
the revolution in the South had partially wrecked the
southern farming landscape. Tens of thousands of
slaves had been taken from southern farms and
plantations by both British forces and Loyalists. In
Georgia and South Carolina, the rice fields had been
neglected, their dikes having collapsed, causing a
steep decline in rice production. (The 1783 crop, for
instance, was half that of 1782.) Indigo, a plant used to
produce a deep blue dye, and its cultivation was nearly
ended in South Carolina and Georgia as cheaper East
Indian indigo became available. Tobacco had provided
a "cash crop" for many southerners since the early
days of Jamestown. However, it too no longer
generated great profits. Warehouses were full of
tobacco by the 1790s, both in America and abroad. In

addition, the growing of tobacco had sapped the nutrients out of the soil of southern farms. As white farmers and plantation owners shifted away from tobacco production to growing corn or wheat—two crops that did not require nine months of intense cultivation—owning slaves proved less profitable. By the 1790s, the southern economy was in desperate need of a new cash crop. Such a crop would bring back a new level of prosperity to southerners and, perhaps, allow slavery to pay greater dividends, as it had in early decades and centuries.[1]

The Invention of the Cotton Gin

In 1793, however, the future of southern agriculture changed. A northerner named Eli Whitney invented a device called the cotton gin, which removed the sticky, green seeds found in cotton. These bothersome seeds were described by one observer as "covered with a kind of green coat resembling velvet."[2] This simple, hand-cranked machine changed the future of American slavery. Cotton production had always been kept to a minimum because, while the Southern climate could easily support cotton, the crop was extremely labor intensive. Cotton seeds were difficult to remove by hand. A field laborer could easily pick fifty pounds of cotton bolls in a day. But seed removal from that amount of cotton might take a single worker nearly a month. This bottleneck in the production of useable cotton lint to make thread made cotton cultivation not very profitable. That is, until Eli Whitney's new invention.

Whitney's device was very efficient. A pair of wooden rollers was grooved lengthwise, and a hand crank turned the rollers in opposite directions. Rows of wire teeth separated the cotton fiber from its seeds. A slotted iron guard contained slits wide enough for the rows of teeth to pass through, along with the cotton fibers they pulled through. But the slits were too narrow to allow the seeds to pass, which further separated them from the fibers, dropping them into a box below the roller. In writing later about his invention, Whitney stated:

> I made a [model] . . . which required the labour of one man to turn it and with which one man will clean ten times as much cotton as he can in any other way before known and also clean it much better than the usual mode. This machine may be turned by water or with a horse, with the greatest ease, and one man and a horse will do more than fifty men with the old machines.[3]

Eli Whitney's invention caused many southerners to embrace slavery even more. Because the seeds could now be separated quickly, even more workers were needed to harvest the crop. By the early 1800s, cotton could be grown across most of the South.[4]

It took only a few slaves to operate a cotton gin on a plantation. However, it took many more to harvest the vast amounts of cotton from the fields.

Slavery Extends Across the West

While the price of cotton never remained stable during the nineteenth century, it was very profitable. However, many workers were still needed to pick the cotton. Slaves spoke of "chopping cotton," which referred to hoeing the weeds. As late as 1850, southern agriculture only invested about 6 percent of its available farmland in cotton production. But those acres required 70 percent more labor to maintain than did an equal acreage of corn.

With the growth of cotton production in the South,

slavery produced great profits. As a result, the value of slaves increased dramatically throughout the early nineteenth century. Between 1800 and 1860, the value of a prime slave field hand increased by twenty-fold. Although the United States banned the international slave trade in 1808, slaves were still bought and sold in the slave markets in America. This resulted in the sale of over eight hundred thousand slaves in America between 1790 and 1860. Many of these slaves were "sold South," and put to work on the ever-expanding cotton fields.[5]

These significant changes caused a major transition across the South in the period between 1790 and 1830. Slavery was once again thriving. A new staple crop (cotton) was dominating southern agriculture. A larger number of white southerners became slave-holders, and many older, traditional slave owners were moving to the newly opened lands to the west, including Alabama, Mississippi, Louisiana, Texas, Arkansas, and western Tennessee. Of the 2.5 million slaves in the United States employed in agriculture in 1860, more than 1.8 million of them were put to work in cotton fields. (The total slave population in America in 1860 was nearly 4 million.)[6] The southern economy rested on a huge bed of cotton.

It was the value of the cotton that caused the South to stake their entire economy on the fibrous commodity.

The profits caused southerners to move west. Thousands of people poured into these territories, speeding along the process of creating new states. Mississippi became a state in 1817, and Alabama followed two years later.[7] Slavery was becoming increasingly a southern institution and less a national one.

The Conditions of Nineteenth-Century Slavery

The average slave owner was not a wealthy individual. However, most slaves lived on larger plantations, because such systems employed more slaves than the average small farm. The result was that many slaves experienced life under the direction of some of the oldest families of the American South. Such slave owners often saw themselves as representing the upper tier of southern society. Their approach to their slaves was often one of paternalism.[8]

This view of slavery developed more fully during the first half of the nineteenth century as a response to criticisms of slaveholding by a growing movement of abolitionists. (Abolitionists believed that slavery should be abolished, or ended.) Paternalism centered on the slave master's view that he was the parent, and his slaves were his "children," regardless of their ages. A common phrase used by slave owners to describe their relationship with their slaves was, "my family, white and black."[9] They believed that all their slaves were dependent on them for their livelihood and that, as such, their responsibility to their slaves was great. With this view, such slave owners believed that they looked on their slaves with affection. This is clear in the writing of one Louisiana planter who lamented the death of one of his slaves who had served as plantation manager:

> Now my heart is nearly broke. I have lost poor Leven, one of the most faithful black men [that] ever lived. [H]e was truth and honesty, and without a fault that I ever

Working the cotton fields was hard work in the hot sun. Slaves often suffered from crippling back pain due to the constant bending over that was required.

discovered. He has overseed the plantation nearly three years, and [has] done much better than any white man [had] ever done here.[10]

While they still intended for their slaves to know their role and keep "in their place," some masters were incapable of understanding why anyone would criticize the slave system. Others used the idea of paternalism as an excuse to justify slavery.

Yet, despite such attitudes from white owners, slaves led difficult lives filled with sorrow, poverty, and hard work. They were provided the necessities, but they were few and simple. The slave diet was basic, typically including corn or cornmeal, fat pork or fish, molasses, and coffee. Slaves might enjoy fresh vegetables that they often had to grow themselves, but they consumed these so rarely that vitamin deficiencies were extremely common among slave populations.[11]

The slave's clothing was simple and rough. A slave might wear the same clothing during an entire year and, perhaps, could expect a new outfit at Christmastime. Slave clothing was often made from osnaburg, a coarse, durable material of light cotton. Slaves despised the rough clothing. Said one Virginia slave: "Dat ole nigger-cloth was jus' like needles when it was new. Never did have to scratch our back. Jus' wriggle yo' shoulders an' yo' back was scratched."[12] Shoes were nearly non-existent among slaves. The lack of shoes caused many slaves to suffer with such foot ailments as hookworm.

While the clothing allowance for slaves varied from one master to the next, one source, a manual used on a plantation owned by James H. Hammond, described those items provided to his slaves:

Each man gets in the fall 2 shirts of cotton drilling, a pair of woolen pants and a woolen jacket. In the spring 2 shirts of cotton shirting and 2 pr. of cotton pants. . . . Each woman gets. . . . In the spring 6 yds. of cotton shirting and 6 yds. of cotton cloth similar to that for men's pants, needle thread and buttons. Each worker gets a stout pr. of shoes every fall, and a heavy blanket every third year.[13]

Slave cabins were small and drafty, hot in the summer and cold in the winter. Such quarters were usually only one room with a dirt floor, a small number of furnishings, and mattresses stuffed with straw or corn shucks. It was not uncommon for two slave families to share a cabin. In such close quarters, diseases were easily passed from one person to the next.[14]

The order of every day for the slave was hard work. Often, a slave was only given one day a year off—Christmas. The slave's workday began at sunrise and ended at sunset. This schedule of working "sun to sun" was typical across the South. Slave owners paid a significant amount of money for many of their slaves.

Slave cabins were often small. This cabin—located at Bass Place, near Columbus, Georgia—was photographed in 1936.

(Children born to slaves became the slaves of their parents' masters.) The owners expected to squeeze as much work out of their "investment" as possible. Fieldwork was not reserved just for men, either. Slave women were expected to work in the fields, even when pregnant.[15]

Slave owners used discipline to keep their workers in line and productive. Such discipline was usually quick and designed to teach a lesson without damaging the slave so severely that he or she could not work. This was the general practice, but some slave owners treated their slaves with an additional dose of cruelty. Such abusive owners might whip their slaves dozens of times, creating extensive blistering on their victims' backs. Then the owner might drip hot sealing wax or throw salt or pepper into the wounds to add to the slave's agony. People told stories of pregnant slaves who received a whipping. Holes were dug to accommodate their stomachs as they were laid on the ground before the whip delivered its harsh blows. Other forms of slave punishment included mutilations, burnings and scaldings, tortures, and even murders.[16]

Despite, or perhaps because of, the constant threat of severe punishments, slaves revolted occasionally. In the summer of 1800, a group of slaves met and planned an assault on Richmond, Virginia. Several of the conspirators were slaves whose masters allowed them to meet with fellow slaves and travel regularly. One of them, a blacksmith named Gabriel Prosser, was even literate. Prosser and his followers spent months lining up slave supporters for their plan. They intended to seize Virginia's state arsenal and kidnap the governor, James Monroe, who later became president of the United States. They hoped that their success would lead others to join them and spread the rebellion even further. Several hundred slaves agreed to follow Prosser and his colleagues and a date was set for the rebellion. But before the elaborate revolt plan could take place, other slaves informed their owners

SOURCE DOCUMENT

De overseers was terrible hard on us. Dey'd ride up and down de field and haste you so till you near about fell out. Sometimes and most generally every time you behind the crowd you got a good lickin' with de bull-whip dat de driver had in de saddle with him. I heard Mammy say dat one day dey whipped poor Leah till she fall out like she was dead. Den dey rubbed salt and pepper on de blisters to make 'em burn real good. She was so sore till she couldn't lay on her back nights, and she just couldn't stand for no clothes to touch her back whatsoever.[17]

Mary Ella Grandberry, a former slave, described the harsh treatment the field hands received on the cotton plantation. Grandberry was interviewed in the late 1930s at the age of ninety. This means that she was a teenager when the slaves were freed shortly after the Civil War.

of the plot. Warned in turn, Governor Monroe called out the state militia, who put down the rebellion. (A heavy thunderstorm the night of the planned attack also kept conspirators from joining together.) Twenty of the conspirators were executed, including Prosser.[18]

Another elaborate plot was hatched by slaves in Charleston, South Carolina, in 1822. It was conceived by a former slave, Denmark Vesey. A literate carpenter, he was inspired by antislavery speeches made in the U.S. Congress that he had read. Vesey recruited other blacks, both slaves and freemen, convincing them that they could take over the city of Charleston. At least eighty blacks conspired to join Vesey's scheme. Vesey assigned various participants to capture the city's municipal buildings and the town arsenal. But, just as with Prosser's planned rebellion, some slaves informed their masters of the plot, and the state militia moved in to put down the slave conspiracy. Thirty-five black conspirators, including Denmark Vesey, were tried and executed. Thirty-seven more were banished from South Carolina.[19]

The Missouri Compromise

As the number of slaves in the South increased during the first twenty years of the 1800s,

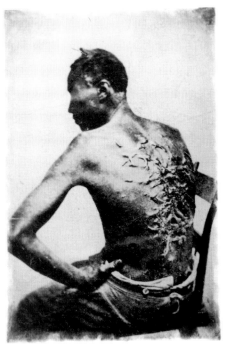

Slaves often bore the scars of severe beatings. Owners saw these beatings as justifiable punishment, while slaves saw them as reason to run, resist, or rebel.

more and more slave territories and states were added to the Union. Many northerners became concerned about the future of free labor in America. Others began to consider the moral implications of slavery.

During the period from 1820 until the beginning of the Civil War forty years later, the primary political issue was the expansion of slavery. In 1819, a storm of concern swirled around the application of yet another territory to enter the Union as a slave state. The territory was Missouri, and the controversy was centered on the movement of slavery out of the Deep South, the traditional southern region stretching from the Chesapeake Bay to the Mississippi River. With Missouri's application, the possibilities were now open for slavery to expand across the entire western region of the Louisiana Purchase territory, a huge landmass of more than eight hundred thousand square miles of the West. Many Northern politicians believed that once slavery was allowed to extend into this vast territory, they would be outnumbered by Southern politicians from the slave-holding states.

Northern politicians simply added up the numbers. Before 1820, five new slave states had been added to the Union: Kentucky, Tennessee, Louisiana, Mississippi, and Alabama. This had established a balance of power in the U.S. Senate, with eleven free states and eleven slave states. (Each state is represented

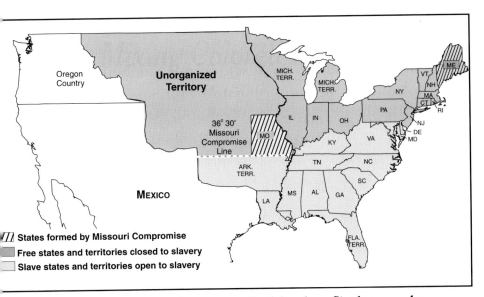

The Missouri Compromise temporarily delayed conflict between the slave and free states.

equally in the Senate by two senators.) With Missouri entering as a slave state, the balance in the Senate would be tilted. Battle lines in Congress were quickly drawn.[20] White southerners were outraged, saying slavery should not be limited there. One southern leader, Thomas Ritchie, warned: "If we yield now, beware. [The North] will ride us forever." Some even talked of leaving the Union, others of civil war.[21] Many northerners were equally emotional. They argued that national policy, dating back to the 1780s and the Articles of Confederation government, had limited slavery by establishing the territory as slave-free under the Northwest Ordinance.

The Senate finally voted, by a narrow margin, for Missouri to enter the Union as a slave state, but only while they voted in Maine as a free state. Kentucky Representative Henry Clay pushed the proposal through the House, seeing to its passage. But another part of this "Missouri Compromise" was important to its passage. Clay had proposed that, regarding the future possibilities of more slave states being carved out of the Louisiana Territory, a line be drawn at the 36 degrees, 30 minutes north latitude (the southern border of Missouri). North of that line, no new slave states would be allowed. (Missouri would be the only slave state that could exist above the line.) The balance of slave and free states was maintained, and the crisis passed—at least for the moment.[22]

ABOLITION AND EMANCIPATION

T HE UNITED STATES BEGAN TO WITNESS THE
serious rumblings of an antislavery movement
by the 1820s. Black abolitionists took the lead in
opposing slavery during this period. Such men as
Samuel Cornish, a Presbyterian minister, became
influential voices. Along with another black
abolitionist, John Russwurm, he began publishing the
first African-American newspaper, *Freedom's Journal*,
in 1827. (Russwurm was a graduate of Bowdoin
College.) The *Journal* encouraged blacks to educate
one another, to rally for their civil rights in the North,
and call for the abolition of slavery.[1]

Several early and influential black abolitionists
were Christian ministers. The preacher Richard Allen
served as the pastor of the Bethel Church of
Philadelphia, a congregation of the African Methodist

Episcopal Church. He founded a school in Philadelphia for black children. He wrote against slavery and opened his home to runaway slaves. Another abolitionist churchman was Absalom Jones, pastor of the St. Thomas Episcopal Church of Philadelphia. In 1797, Jones became the first black leader to petition the U.S. Congress, calling for the abolition of slavery. Both Allen and Jones had been slaves and each had purchased his freedom.[2]

Such abolitionists, while opposed to slavery, were commonly united in opposition to another newly-formed institution—the American Colonization Society (ACS). Following the American Revolution, the idea of returning freed slaves back to Africa began to take form. In 1816, a white clergyman named Robert Finley founded the ACS. The society hoped to draw the support of influential and prominent blacks. By 1822, the ACS established a colony for freed slaves called Liberia on the west coast of Africa. By 1865, more than ten thousand black American colonists had settled there. But, generally, black leaders did not support the colonization effort and spoke out constantly against the American Colonization Society.[3] They opposed the ACS because many of its members believed that if free blacks left the United States, the institution of slavery would be strengthened.

Not all abolitionists were content to call for a legal

end to slavery. Another black abolitionist was David Walker, a resident of Boston. Walker had been born in North Carolina, the son of a slave father. But his mother had been free, so Walker was also born free. Walker developed strong opinions on the subject of slavery and supported the idea of a slave rebellion. In September 1829, he published his *Appeal to the Colored Citizens of the World*, which called for slaves to use violence to overthrow their owners. The appeal was distributed to a wide audience, even reaching southern slaves. Walker's words were clear and forceful: "Remember Americans, that we must and shall be free and enlightened as you are, will you wait until we shall, under God, obtain our liberty by the crushing arm of power? Will it not be dreadful for you?"[4] But a large or far-reaching slave revolt did not take place.[5]

Black women were also important in the abolitionist movement. One such female voice was Charlotte Forten, the wife of the abolitionist leader, James Forten, who, in 1813, had spoken to the Senate of Pennsylvania in opposition to slavery.[6] Charlotte and other black women founded the Philadelphia Female Anti-Slavery Society in 1833. She was strongly opposed to slavery and campaigned fearlessly against the institution and its evils. Charlotte was once quoted saying: "I crave anti-slavery food continually."[7]

Whites also provided leadership in the antislavery

movement of the early nineteenth century. A white leader in that early movement was a Massachusetts native named William Lloyd Garrison. Garrison began publishing his own antislavery publication, *The Liberator*, in Boston on January 1, 1831.

In the first issue of *The Liberator*, Garrison made his position clear, stating: "I will be as harsh as truth, and as uncompromising as justice. On this subject, I do not wish to think, or speak, or write, with moderation. . . . I am in earnest—I will not equivocate—I will not excuse—I will not retreat a single inch—AND I WILL BE HEARD."[8] To many, Garrison became the great symbol, the embodiment of the abolition movement in America. Through the years between 1830 and 1850, the abolitionist movement became one of the most popular reform movements in the country.

Abolitionism

The antislavery movement took the direction of such strong leaders as black abolitionists Frederick Douglass, Sojourner Truth, Robert Purvis, Martin Delany, and others. Influential men like Frederick Douglass wrote and spoke eloquently against slavery. Douglass had been born into slavery in Maryland. At age twenty, he escaped with the help of his master's wife. He went to New York City and married a free black woman he had met in Baltimore. Within a few years, he was speaking to antislavery groups. Douglass wrote his autobiography, titled, *Narrative of the Life of Frederick Douglass*. His story included passages concerning the kind of treatment he received as a young slave:

> In hottest summer and coldest winter, I was kept almost naked—no shoes, no stockings, no jacket, no trousers, nothing on but a coarse tow linen shirt, reaching only to my knees. I had no bed. I must have perished with cold, but that, the coldest nights, I used to steal a bag which was used for carrying corn to the mill. I would crawl into this bag, and there sleep on the cold, damp, clay floor, with my head in and feet out. My feet have been so cracked with the frost, that the pen with which I am writing might be laid in the gashes.[9]

White antislavery supporters, such as Garrison, Benjamin Lundy, Wendell Phillips, Lyman Beecher, and the Grimke sisters took frightening dimensions to those who supported slavery. Slave advocates believed that such talk could inspire slaves to rise up against their masters. Without

Frederick Douglass was a leading voice for the abolition of slavery in the nation.

question, unrest among slaves did increase during the late 1820s and early 1830s, likely inspired by David Walker's *Appeal.*[10] Such antislavery publications were in circulation in the South, especially among free black people. In August 1831, a Virginia slave, Nat Turner, led a rebellion that rallied dozens of slaves to murder fifty-seven whites, including women and children. Southerners blamed Garrison and others for causing the uprising.[11]

The 1840s witnessed fragmentation within the antislavery movement. During the annual meeting of the American Antislavery Society in New York City in 1840, members fell into a squabble over the right of women to hold leadership roles within the movement. Before the meeting ended, a faction of the group walked out. Following this action, no single antislavery society spoke for the movement.

The abolitionist movement, although never accepted by a majority of even northerners, did manage to make inroads in the minds of many. While many northerners remained convinced that blacks were inferior to whites, more northerners had become opponents of slavery by the 1840s.[12]

During the 1830s, as William Lloyd Garrison published *The Liberator*, some southerners responded with an equal amount of passion. In January 1837, one such slavery supporter was a United States senator

Nat Turner's rebellion led to more restrictive laws against slaves. This drawing of the rebellion was made by a white artist. The artist emphasized the brutality of the rebellion in order to promote slavery.

from South Carolina, John C. Calhoun. Calhoun had served as Andrew Jackson's first vice president. Calhoun made his position on the issue of slavery clear by writing the following:

> I hold that in the present state of civilization, where two races of different origin, and distinguished by color and other physical differences, as well as intellectual, are brought together, the relation now existing in the slave-holding states between the two is, instead of an evil, a good—a positive good.

Calhoun's position was based in a firm belief that blacks were inferior to whites.[13]

Slavery and the Power of Congress

By the late 1840s, much of the debate in the United States Congress was no longer about the expansion of slavery. Some congressmen now questioned whether the U.S. Congress had the power to limit where slavery existed at all. Antislavery and proslavery supporters approached the issue from completely different perspectives. Such men as John C. Calhoun believed it was up to each state legislature to determine whether slavery was to exist in its state. In Calhoun's mind, prior to statehood, all territories must be open to slavery.

Northerners opposed to the expansion of slavery believed the Constitution empowered Congress to determine the future scope of the institution. They took the Constitution's assurance that Congress had the power to "make all needful rules and regulations respecting the Territory or other property belonging to the United States" as a mandate allowing the government to set the boundaries of slavery.[14] In addition, most northerners argued that the question of the power of Congress to limit slavery had already been answered. The proof was in such laws as the Ordinance of 1787, which banned slavery from the territories of the Old Northwest, as well as the Missouri Compromise.

The Underground Railroad

By the 1830s and 1840s, slave escapes were happening at the rate of hundreds, even thousands per year. Escape usually took place through the system known as the Underground Railroad. The Underground Railroad was not actually a railroad at all. It was a system of safehouses, called "stations," with sympathetic individuals, called "conductors," hiding and helping escaped slaves on their journey north. Exactly when the Underground Railroad began is impossible to date. By the 1840s, a system was in place that included moving slaves across the Tidewater states of Virginia and Maryland, as well as Kentucky and Missouri. The end of the "Underground Railroad" line was ultimately Canada.[15]

Many stories of slaves who escaped along one part or another of the Underground Railroad were recorded. They often include narrow escapes, elaborate deceptions, and tense moments. The stations along the Underground Railroad were often close to each other, usually ten or twenty miles apart. During the day, escaped slaves could rest at the stations, get a meal, and directions where to move to next up the line. Such slaves were hidden in cellars, attics, and barns and other outbuildings.[16]

Those who participated in helping slaves escape did so at great risk. One of the most famous Underground Railroad conductors was a former slave named Harriet Tubman. Born in 1820, Tubman escaped from a Maryland plantation in 1849 after her abusive owner threatened to sell her and her family to

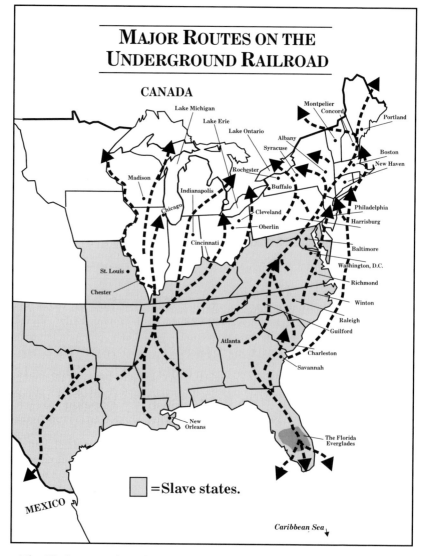

The Underground Railroad's complex network ensured that a slave from almost any part of the South could be helped to freedom.

a plantation "down south." (The slavery practiced further south was often more abusive than in the Upper South.) After her own escape, she helped other slaves escape secretly, returning fifteen times to Maryland. Despite the challenges and risks, many people who believed slavery was wrong participated in the Underground Railroad. Historians estimate that more than thirty-two hundred people worked actively in helping move slaves to northern freedom. One man especially, a white Quaker named Levi Coffin, is remembered for his commitment to helping free slaves. From his home in Newport, Indiana, he helped as many as three thousand slaves escape.

A New Fugitive Slave Law

As the slaves moved into northern states, they were not legally free, but most state officials increasingly looked the other way. Some states

Harriet Tubman was called Moses by the slaves she helped. This referred to a man in the Bible named Moses who led his people out of slavery.

even passed personal liberty laws to help escaped slaves. The Fugitive Slave Law of 1850 was designed to change all that. Under the law, any slave captured in the North was to be returned to the South. All state officials and private citizens were required to aid in the recovery of escaped slaves. Anyone refusing to participate in slave recovery was liable for paying a stiff fine and might face jail time. The Fugitive Slave Law of 1850 drew many emotional, highly charged responses, primarily from northerners. Northern cities witnessed several riots in protest of the federal action. Some northern mobs actually broke into jails and freed fugitives before they could be returned to their lives as slaves in the South.[17]

Uncle Tom's Cabin

The law also caused an action of an extremely different kind. In 1852, a forty-one-year-old woman from Maine, Harriet Beecher Stowe, published a work called *Uncle Tom's Cabin, or Life Among the Lowly*. The book was intended as an antislavery novel. No one could have predicted the impact this single literary work would have on the American public and its opinions concerning slavery. *Uncle Tom's Cabin* featured memorable characters who gave the reader a more personal, emotional picture of what southern slavery was sometimes about. The book's sympathetic slave images—especially of the slave girl, Eliza, as she escapes slavery by crossing the ice-choked Ohio River, with a slave catcher hot on her heels—caused many who read the work to come to a personal conclusion about the sin and immorality of slavery.

Uncle Tom's Cabin was an instant success. In book form, the work sold five thousand copies in two days and ten times that number in two months. A year after publication, three hundred thousand copies had been sold; by 1854, the book had sold more than 1 million copies, making it the best-selling book of nineteenth century America. It also sold many copies abroad. Great Britain's Queen Victoria is said to have wept after reading the American story.[18]

The Kansas-Nebraska Controversy
On January 4, 1854, Illinois senator Stephen Douglas introduced a bill calling for the organization of the Nebraska Territory, which covered lands much larger than the state of Nebraska today. Douglas had his own agenda in establishing an organized Nebraska Territory. He had a strong interest in establishing a northern route for any possible transcontinental railroad from the Eastern United States to California. As a senator from Illinois and chairman of the Senate Committee on Territories, Douglas wanted to see the mid-western terminus of the railroad established in

Chicago. Otherwise, the territorial organization would encourage settlement of Americans across the Great Plains.[19]

As Douglas wrote the Nebraska bill, he needed support from southern Democrats. Southern senators demanded that Douglas include a clause calling for the repeal of the Missouri Compromise and the opening of slavery into the territory north of the 36 degrees, 30 minutes parallel. (Slavery had been banned there under the Missouri Compromise.) Douglas's bill included an approach to slavery called "popular sovereignty." This political idea left the decision of whether a territory (and later a state) would have slavery up to the people living there.

Douglas accommodated his critics by writing popular sovereignty in his proposed legislation. In the final version of the bill, Douglas divided the northern lands in question into both the Nebraska and Kansas territories. Southerners assumed that the Nebraska territory would remain free and that Kansas, just west of a slave state, Missouri, would become a slave state itself. The Kansas-Nebraska bill resulted in a loud debate in Congress, yet it passed in 1854. The act destroyed the old Missouri Compromise, opening up northern territory to the possibilities of slavery.[20]

Once the Kansas-Nebraska Act passed, the race was soon on between proslavery and antislavery advocates to organize a territorial government in Kansas. Beginning in 1854 and for the next six years, the Kansas Territory was a battleground, as slavery's advocates and detractors fought one another over the political future of the new western lands.

Violence Across Kansas

Waves of violence broke out across Kansas. An antislavery man in Leavenworth was attacked by a mob of proslavery advocates who hacked at him with knives and hatchets, leaving him to die. Then, a proslavery sheriff was shot and killed while he and a group of men attempted to arrest six antislavery men for "contempt of court."

This era of "Bleeding Kansas" continued into 1856. That year, a group of proslavery men sacked the antislavery town of Lawrence, Kansas. Eight hundred proslavery supporters entered the antislavery community in search of the leaders of the antislavery government. The posse burned the local lodging establishment, called the Free Soil Hotel, looted houses and destroyed two antislavery printing presses. One man was killed. That raid brought a response from John Brown, an intensely driven abolitionist. Brown and his supporters attacked and murdered five proslavery settlers in the settlement of Potowatomie Creek.[21]

The Marais des Cygnes massacre of antislavery advocates was just one of the many acts of violence during the long-standing conflict known as "Bleeding Kansas."

As these events took place in Kansas, another act of violence was taking place in the nation's capitol. On May 29, 1856, a senator from Massachusetts, Charles Sumner, was beaten nearly to death by a South Carolina representative named Preston Brooks. Sumner had angered Brooks during a speech in which Sumner was highly critical of the South's continuing support of slavery. He had also condemned Brook's uncle, Senator Andrew Pickens Butler. Violence over slavery had found its way into the halls of American government.[22]

The Case of Dred Scott

As late as 1856, the issue of whether the United States Congress retained the power to limit the expansion of slavery into any territory had never been fully answered. Now, the United States Supreme Court had made the decision for the entire country. The case was to be known as *Dred Scott* v. *Sandford.*

Dred Scott, a Missouri slave, filed a suit demanding his freedom. He claimed to be free because his owner had taken him outside slave territory during the 1830s. His master, an army surgeon named Emerson, had lived four years in Illinois, a free state, then Wisconsin, a free territory. During those years, Dred Scott's lawyer argued, he had been free because slavery did not exist in either Illinois or Wisconsin. In 1856, the case was heard before the Supreme Court. Then, in March 1857, by a margin of 7–2, the Court ruled against Dred Scott. The Chief Justice, Roger B. Taney, writing the majority decision, stated that Scott could not legally sue in court because he was a slave. Taney declared that black persons, whether slave or free, could not be recognized as citizens of the United States, because the writers of the United States Constitution had not defined them as "the people" or "citizens." Taney wrote in his decision that blacks "had for more than a century been regarded as beings of an inferior order . . . so far inferior that they had no rights which white men were bound to respect."[23]

In addition, Taney stated that the Missouri Compromise was, indeed, unconstitutional. He added that Congress was not empowered to limit where slavery existed. The Dred Scott decision was a powerful setback for the antislavery movement and for anyone who believed in the limiting of slavery to a specific region of the country. The new equation for blacks was obvious. Even free blacks had no legitimate, legal rights.[24]

Few blacks saw anything positive in the Dred Scott decision. The famous abolitionist Frederick Douglass, who had escaped slavery as a young man, was one. He wrote that the decision was such an outrageous one that it might represent "one necessary link in the chain of events [leading] to the complete overthrow of the whole slave system."[25]

John Brown's Raid

Throughout the 1850s, events seemed to point in one direction: The widening split between the supporters of slavery and those who opposed it. In the late fall of 1859, antislavery fanatics bent on the destruction of the institution raided a federal arsenal.

The leader of the raid was John Brown. He and his followers planned to attack the federal arsenal at Harpers Ferry, Virginia, capture a large supply of muskets, and take up refuge in the Allegheny mountains. (Today, Harpers Ferry is in West Virginia.) There, they would call for a general slave rebellion to bring an end to the hated institution.

On the evening of October 16, 1859, Brown and about twenty-one others, both blacks and whites, drove an old wagon loaded with two hundred rifles and two hundred revolvers toward the sleepy Virginia town. Brown and his men, including several of his own sons, seized the arsenal and its armory. Raiding parties were then sent out to free local slaves and to take hostages. Later that night, someone rang a church bell, warning the local citizens that a slave rebellion was underway. Militia units began to arrive. Hopelessly trapped, Brown sent out men carrying white flags, intending to surrender. Both times, the men were fired on and killed.

By the morning of October 18, U.S. Marines arrived and stormed a firehouse where Brown and his men had taken refuge. The abolitionist was taken prisoner, along with six of his men. Brown and his colleagues then stood trial for treason against the state of Virginia. Brown was hanged in December. As he climbed to the gallows, he handed a note to one of his guards: "I, John Brown, am now quite certain that the crimes of this guilty land will never be purged away but with blood." Some northern political leaders, such as Abraham Lincoln, made it clear that they did not condone the actions of Brown. Lincoln called the Harpers

Ferry raid an act of "violence, bloodshed, and treason." But many white southerners refused to believe Lincoln's words.[26]

The following year—1860—the presidential election determined the direction of the entire country. The Democratic party nominated Senator Stephen Douglas as their candidate. But Southern Democrats found Douglas unacceptable, due to his support of popular sovereignty. They selected their own candidate, a Kentuckian named John C. Breckinridge, who demanded a federal code to protect slavery in the territories. Breckinridge's extremism may have directly pushed the Republicans to nominate a candidate who might not appear offensive or radical to southerners: Abraham Lincoln. Yet a fourth candidate was also nominated, John Bell from Tennessee. His support came from a coalition group called the Constitutional Union party, largely southerners who feared the division of the Union and secession, or separation, of the Southern states.

When the election was held on November 6, 1860, the votes were cast generally along sectional lines. Northerners voted for Lincoln, with the Illinois candidate capturing 180 electoral votes, almost 50 percent more than his three political rivals combined. With Lincoln's election win, the southern states believed that their hopes for gaining any further ground for

Abraham Lincoln at first went to war to save the Union, not to free the slaves. However, after a vast number of slaves ran away and joined the Union lines, he began to change his mind.

the advancement and protection of slavery were gone. Within weeks of the election, states began the bitter process of secession.

Slavery and the Civil War

By April 1861, the Civil War began following a Confederate attack on Fort Sumter, situated in the harbor at Charleston, South Carolina. By that time, seven southern states—South Carolina, Mississippi, Alabama, Georgia, Florida, Texas, and Louisiana—had left the union and formed the Confederate States of America. After Fort Sumter, four more southern states—North Carolina, Virginia, Tennessee, and Arkansas—also left the United States. These eleven states intended to establish their own country, one in which slavery and the states' rights to govern themselves would always be protected.

President Abraham Lincoln was determined not to

allow these southern states to separate from the United States, and he was willing to fight to hold them in the Union. As the Civil War opened, most northerners were prepared to fight for maintaining the Union. They were not interested in fighting to end slavery. Reuniting the country once again would remain a goal of the Lincoln administration and most of Lincoln's fellow northerners during the war.

During the early years of the war, black recruits for Union military service were rejected. Although thousands of blacks were prepared to put on a blue uniform and fight in the spring of 1861, the Secretary of War, Simon Cameron, was not prepared to allow blacks to serve. The black community felt frustrated at this early rejection. As a writer for a black New York newspaper wrote: "We are concerned in this fight and our fate hangs upon its issues. The South must be subjugated, or we shall be enslaved."[27]

The Confiscation Acts of 1861 and 1862

Members of the Lincoln administration, including President Lincoln himself, were not prepared to take serious steps concerning the institution of slavery early in the war. However, Congress did pass two important pieces of legislation called Confiscation Acts. The first was passed in August 1861. It defined the status of all escaped slaves who made their way behind Union lines. Such escaped slaves were not automatically freed. However, those who had been employed by the Confederate Army were allowed to remain in Union hands as "contraband of war."

The second Confiscation Act was passed nearly a year later, in July 1862. This act designated that all slaves confiscated within the borders of the Confederate states would be freed. However, the act was never fully enforced.[28]

The Emancipation Proclamation

However, despite Lincoln's early opposition to making slavery a major cause for the northern war effort, by the summer of 1862 he began changing his mind. During April and June, he had watched Congress abolish slavery in the District of Columbia and in the western territories. Both steps encouraged Lincoln to take his own initiatives. To one of his cabinet members, Lincoln said: "We must free the slaves or be ourselves subdued. The slaves were undeniably an element of strength to those who had their service, and we must decide whether that element should be with us or against us."[29] When Lincoln met with his cabinet in late July 1862, only his postmaster general was opposed to emancipation of southern slaves.[30]

That fall, Abraham Lincoln issued a presidential announcement called the Emancipation Proclamation.

Slated to take effect on January 1, 1863, Lincoln's proclamation stated any slave held in states in rebellion against the United States would be "thenceforward, and forever free."

When New Year's Day, 1863, arrived, blacks and many whites across the divided country celebrated enthusiastically. A large group of rejoicers, including Frederick Douglass, William Lloyd Garrison, and Harriet Beecher Stowe, met in Tremont Temple in Boston to mark the end of slavery in the Confederate states. Douglass described the scene: "Joy and gladness exhausted all forms of expression, from shouts of praise to sobs and tears."[31] Finally, after nearly 250 years in North America, the institution took its most serious blow.

In addition, once the Emancipation Proclamation was issued, the way was prepared for blacks to be included in the Union army. However, some black soldiers had already served in the Union Army even before Lincoln's announcement. In May 1862, former slaves had been recruited in South Carolina and organized into a five-hundred-man unit called the First South Carolina Volunteers.[32]

One of the first black units formed in the north included free black men and would eventually become the most famous black fighting regiment of the Civil War—the 54th Massachusetts Regiment. Formed in January 1863 by the governor of Massachusetts, the

African-American soldiers gave their lives to help turn the tide of the Civil War.

54th was organized with the help of important black leaders, such as Frederick Douglass. Two of Douglass's sons served in the ranks of the 54th. The regiment was commanded by a white officer named Robert Shaw. So many free blacks enlisted into the ranks of the Massachusetts 54th that another unit, the 55th Massachusetts, was formed, as well as the 5th Massachusetts Cavalry Regiment.[33]

Throughout the last two years of the war, more than one hundred eighty-six thousand blacks enlisted in support of the Union war effort. Of that number, approximately half came from the secession states of the Confederacy. Another forty thousand were from the border-slave states. Approximately one out of every four was a northern black. Black Union soldiers participated in the fighting in every part of the country. These troops risked everything to fight. Some of them were captured by the Confederates and sold into slavery. Some were killed even after they surrendered.

Others were held as prisoners of war and forced to work building rebel fortifications. A total of thirty-eight thousand blacks lost their lives during their military service.[34]

The End of American Slavery

By the end of 1863, the Republican-controlled U.S. Congress had determined that slavery needed to be dissolved completely. The following April, the Senate passed the Thirteenth Amendment, which called for the abolition of slavery, to the U.S. Constitution. The amendment passed 38 to 6. However, Democrats in the House of Representatives blocked the amendment the following summer. Those longing for slavery's end had to wait until the following session of Congress, after the fall elections, when Republicans gained more seats in the House. But before the vote was taken on January 31, 1865, President Lincoln urged Democratic opponents of the amendment to change their minds and support this important piece of historical legislation. Several did so, including sixteen Democrats who had formerly voted against the Thirteenth Amendment. On the final day of January, the House of Representatives voted 119 to 56 in favor of the new law ending American slavery. It was later ratified and officially became law on December 6, 1865.

On April 14, 1865, Abraham Lincoln was assassinated

by John Wilkes Booth, a southerner. The assassin's coconspirators were hunted, tried, and hanged. Booth was shot and killed by federal troops. A little over a month after Lincoln was killed, the Civil War officially ended on May 26, 1865.

Despite the death of Lincoln, the year 1865 witnessed the great joy felt by blacks across the United States that slavery had finally been destroyed in America. For hundreds of years, slave owners, planters, slave merchants, ship captains, and others

SOURCE DOCUMENT

One day I was out milking the cows. Mr. Dave come down into the field, and he had a paper in his hands. "Listen to me Tom," he said. "Listen to what I reads you." And he read from a paper all about how I was free. You can't tell how I felt. "You're jokin' me," I says. "No, I ain't," says he, "you're free." . . .

Was I happy? Lord! You can take anything. No matter how good you treat it—it wants to be free. You can treat it good and feed it and give it everything it seems to want—but if you open the cage—it's happy . . . [35]

Former slave Tom Robinson described the day he found out he was freed from slavery.

had exploited Africans and those of African descent. Slaves had experienced the indignities of an institution that had considered them inferior. They had endured humiliations, beatings, mistreatment, and lives of endless labor. Their families had been broken up and they had watched their children grow up with no hope of another life.

However, they ran away, revolted, and worked against their masters every day. They had grown in number to four million by the time of the Civil War. And many of them fought against their former oppressors during the war. By the 1860s, the former slaves, whites, and free blacks who spoke out against slavery had finally been heard. It was a new day for blacks in the United States. Decades later, former slave and great African-American leader, Booker T. Washington, spoke about the end of slavery and what it meant for those oppressed millions who could finally taste the fruits of being free:

> As the great day grew nearer, there was more singing in the slave quarters than usual. It was bolder, had more ring, and lasted later into the night. Most of the verses of the plantation songs had some reference to freedom. True, they had sung those same verses before, but they had been careful to explain that the "freedom" in these songs referred to the next world, and had no connection with life in this world. Now they gradually threw off the mask, and were not afraid to let it be known that the "freedom" in their songs meant freedom of the body in this world.[36]

→ T I M E L I N E ←

∙∙∙∙∙∙∙∙∙∙∙∙∙∙∙∙∙∙∙∙∙∙∙∙∙∙∙∙∙ O=×=O ∙∙∙∙∙∙∙∙∙∙∙∙∙∙∙∙∙∙∙∙∙∙∙∙∙∙∙∙∙∙∙

1441 –1448	More than one thousand Africans are imported to Portugal.
1600	Twenty-five thousand Africans are working on plantations in the Caribbean.
1619	A Dutch shipper delivers twenty Africans to the English outpost at Jamestown, Virginia.
1660s	British colonies of North America begin to legally recognize black slavery.
1739	The Stono Rebellion occurs outside Charleston, South Carolina.
1775	*December 30*: General George Washington opens the ranks of the Continental Army to black soldiers.
1784	Every northern state, except for New York and New Jersey, had passed legislation calling for the end of slavery in that state.
1787	The Ordinance of 1787 organizes the Old Northwest Territory without slavery.
1790	Approximately two hundred seventy-five thousand black slaves have been imported into the British colonies of North America.
1793	The U.S. Congress creates a fugitive slave law; Northerner Eli Whitney invents the cotton gin.
1808	The United States government bans the international slave trade.
1820	The Missouri Compromise is enacted.

1830s	Antislavery supporters gradually create a system called the Underground Railroad, designed to help slaves escape to the north.
1831	*January 1*: Abolitionist William Lloyd Garrison begins publishing his antislavery newspaper, *The Liberator*. *August*: Virginia slave Nat Turner leads dozens of slaves in rebellion.
1850	The Compromise of 1850 is passed.
1852	Harriet Beecher Stowe publishes her antislavery novel, *Uncle Tom's Cabin*.
1854	The Kansas-Nebraska Act is passed.
1854 −1860	"Bleeding Kansas" is split between slavery and antislavery supporters.
1857	The Supreme court decision, *Dred Scott* v. *Sandford*, opens up all United States territories to slavery.
1859	*October*: Abolitionist John Brown raids Harpers Ferry arsenal.
1860	The United States is home to 4 million slaves; Republican Abraham Lincoln is elected the sixteenth president.
1861	*April 12*: Civil War begins.
1863	*January 1*: The Emancipation Proclamation goes into effect.
1865	*May 26*: Civil War ends. *December 6*: The Thirteenth Amendment is ratified, ending slavery.

CHAPTER NOTES

CHAPTER 1. THE STORY OF JOSIAH HENSON

1. Abraham Chapman, ed., *Steal Away: Stories of the Runaway Slaves* (New York: Praeger Publishers, 1971), p. 83.

2. Josiah Henson, *The Life of Josiah Henson, Formerly a Slave, Now an Inhabitant of Canada, as Narrated by Himself* (Boston: Arthur D. Phelps, 1849), p. 1.

3. Ibid., p. 7.

4. Ibid., p. 19.

5. Josiah Henson, *"The Life of Josiah Henson, Formerly a Slave, Now an Inhabitant of Canada, as Narrated by Himself,"* The University of North Carolina at Chapel Hill Libraries: Documenting the American South, © 2001, <http://docsouth.unc.edu/neh/henson49/henson49.html> (September 16, 2003).

6. Josiah Henson, *The Life of Josiah Henson, Formerly a Slave, Now an Inhabitant of Canada, as Narrated by Himself* (Boston: Arthur D. Phelps, 1849), pp. 50–51.

7. Chapman, p. 86.

8. Ibid., p. 87.

9. Henson, pp. 51–52.

10. Chapman, p. 89.

11. Henson, pp. 58–59.

12. Ibid., p. 75.

CHAPTER 2. THE SLAVE TRADE

1. Steven Mintz, ed., *African American Voices: The Life Cycle of Slavery* (St. James, N.Y.: Brandywine Press, 1996), pp. 2–3.

2. Darlene Clark Hine, William C. Hine, and Stanley Harrold, *The African-American Odyssey* (Upper Saddle River, N.J.: Prentice Hall, 2002), p. 27.

3. John Hope Franklin, *From Slavery to Freedom* (New York: Alfred A. Knopf, 1967), pp. 62–64.

4. Peter Charles Hoffer, *The Brave New World, A History of Early America* (Boston: Houghton Mifflin Company, 2000), pp. 95, 98.

5. Eric Williams, "The Development of the Negro Slave Trade," *America's Black Past: A Reader in Afro-American History*, Eric Foner, ed. (New York: Harper & Row Publishers, 1970), p. 38.

6. John Hope Franklin, *From Slavery to Freedom: A History of Negro Americans*, 3rd ed. (New York: Alfred A. Knopf, 1967), pp. 26–27.

7. Ibid., pp. 28–31; John Mark Faragher, *Out of Many: A History of the American People* (Upper Saddle River, N.J.: Prentice Hall, 1997), p. 84.

8. Hugh Thomas, *The Slave Trade: The Story of the Atlantic Slave Trade: 1440–1870* (New York: Simon & Schuster, 1997), pp. 44–46.

9. Clifford Lindsey Alderman, *Rum, Slaves and Molasses: The Story of New England's Triangular Trade* (New York: Crowell-Collier Press, 1972), p. 70; Hoffer, p. 95.

10. Ibid., p. 17.

11. Ibid., Faragher, p. 86.

12. Kenneth G. Goode, *From Africa to the United States and Then . . . A Concise Afro-American History* (Glenview, Ill.: Scott, Foresman and Company, 1969), p. 17.

13. William J. Cooper, Jr. and Thomas E. Terrill, *The American South, A History* (New York: Alfred A. Knopf, 1990), p. 49.

14. Alderman, p. 53.

15. Thomas, p. 421; Goode, pp. 18–19.

16. Thomas, pp. 420–421; Goode, pp. 17–18.

17. Alderman, pp. 63–64.

18. Ibid., p. 64.

19. Ibid., pp. 64–65.

CHAPTER 3. SLAVERY IN THE COLONIES

1. John Hope Franklin, *From Slavery to Freedom: A History of Negro Americans,* 3rd ed. (New York: Alfred A. Knopf, 1967), pp. 60–61.

2. Ibid., pp. 61–62.

3. Peter Charles Hoffer, *The Brave New World, A History of Early America* (Boston: Houghton Mifflin Company, 2000), p. 168.

4. Hugh Thomas, *The Slave Trade: The Story of the Atlantic Slave Trade: 1440–1870* (New York: Simon & Schuster, 1997), p. 206.

5. Kenneth G. Goode, *From Africa to the United States and Then . . . A Concise Afro-American History* (Glenview, Ill.: Scott, Foresman and Company, 1969), pp. 21–23.

6. Franklin, p. 63.

7. Clifford Lindsey Alderman, *Rum, Slaves and Molasses: The Story of New England's Triangular Trade* (New York: Crowell-Collier Press, 1972), pp. 75–77.

8. Franklin, p. 62.

9. Goode, p. 22

10. Winthrop D. Jordan, "Unthinking Decision: Enslavement of Negroes in America to 1700," James Kirby Martin, *Interpreting Colonial America, Selected Readings* (New York: Dodd, Mead & Company, 1974), p. 167.

11. Hoffer, pp. 146–147, 152.

12. Alderman, pp. 19–20.

13. Jordan, pp. 167–168.

14. Franklin, pp. 71–72.

15. Jordan, p. 168.

16. Edmund S. Morgan, *American Slavery, American Freedom: The Ordeal of Colonial Virginia.* (New York: W. W. Norton & Company, 1995), pp. 298–299.

17. Richard Hofstadter, *America at 1750, A Social Portrait* (New York: Alfred A. Knopf, 1972), p. 111.

18. Franklin, pp. 76–79, 91–99.

19. Hoffer, pp. 164–65.

20. "Selected Virginia Statutes relating to Slavery," *Virtual Jamestown,* ©Crandall Shifflett All Rights Reserved 1998, <http://www.iath.virginia.edu/vcdh/jamestown/laws1.html#38> (September 16, 2003)

21. Franklin, p. 86.

22. Alderman, pp. 20–21.

23. Ibid., pp. 97–99, 104, 107.

24. Darlene Clark Hine, William C. Hine, and Stanley Harrold, *The African-American Odyssey* (Upper Saddle River, N.J.: Prentice Hall, 2003), pp. 62–63.

25. Ibid., p. 63.

26. Ibid., p. 68.

27. Ibid.

28. Ibid., p. 67.

CHAPTER 4. SLAVERY AND REVOLUTION

1. William J. Cooper, Jr. and Thomas E. Terrill, *The American South, A History* (New York: Alfred A. Knopf, 1990), p. 46.

2. Edgar A. Toppin, "Slavery in the British Colonies, 1619–1763," in *From Freedom to Freedom: African Roots in American Soil,* ed. Mildred Bain and Ervin Lewis (Milwaukee: Purnell Reference Books, 1977), p. 183.

3. Cooper and Terrill, pp. 48–49.

4. Ibid., p. 48.

5. Lisa W. Strick, "The Black Presence in the Revolution, 1770–1800," *From Freedom to Freedom,* Mildred Bain and Ervin Lewis, eds. (Milwaukee: Purnell Reference Books, 1977), p. 213.

6. Darlene Clark Hine, William C. Hine, and Stanley Harrold, *The African-American Odyssey* (Upper Saddle River, N.J.: Prentice Hall, 2002), p. 76.

7. David Brion Davis, *The Problem of Slavery in the Age of Revolution, 1770–1823* (Ithaca, N.Y.: Cornell University Press, 1975), p. 283.

8. David McCullough, *John Adams* (New York: Simon & Schuster, 2001), p. 67.

9. Gary B. Nash, *Race and Revolution* (Madison, Wis.: Madison House, 1990), pp. 173–174.

10. Roy E. Finkenbine, *Sources of the African-American Past, Primary Sources in American History* (New York: Longman, 1997), p. 21.

11. Hine, et. al., p. 84.

12. Robert Middlekauff, *The Glorious Cause: The American Revolution, 1763–1789* (New York: Oxford University Press, 1982), p. 556; Hine, pp. 81–82.

13. Ibid.

14. Hine, et. al., pp. 84–85.

15. "Journals of the Continental Congress: Monday, March 29, 1779," *The Library of Congress*, n.d., <http://memory.loc.gov/cgi-bin/query/D?hlaw:2:./temp/~ammem_IUJ5::> (September 16, 2003).

16. Hine, p. 86.

17. Finkenbine, p. 21.

18. Hine, et. al., p. 87.

19. Ibid., pp. 87–88.

20. Ibid., p. 90.

CHAPTER 5. KING COTTON

1. Constance M. Green, *Eli Whitney and the Birth of American Technology* (New York: Little, Brown and Company, 1956), pp. 6–7.

2. Ibid., p. 46.

3. Ibid.

4. Robert Heilbroner and Aaron Singer, *The Economic Transformation of America, 1600 to the Present*, 3rd ed. (New York: Harcourt Brace, 1994), pp. 131–132.

5. Darlene Clark Hine, William C. Hine, and Stanley Harrold, *The African-American Odyssey* (Upper Saddle River, N.J.: Prentice Hall, 2002), p. 125.

6. Ibid., pp. 127–129.

7. Heilbroner, pp. 131–132.

8. Eugene D. Genovese, *Roll, Jordan, Roll: The World the Slaves Made* (New York: Pantheon Books, 1972), pp. 48–49; Heilbroner and Singer, p. 133.

9. Elizabeth Fox-Genovese, *Within the Plantation Household: Black and White Women of the Old South* (Chapel Hill: University of North Carolina Press, 1988), p. 101.

10. Robert William Fogel and Stanley L. Engerman, *Time on the Cross: The Economics of American Negro Slavery* (Boston: Little, Brown and Company, 1974), p. 77.

11. Heilbroner, p. 133.

12. Hine, et. al., pp. 139; Genovese, p. 551.

13. Kenneth M. Stampp, *The Peculiar Institution: Slavery in the Antebellum South* (New York: Alfred A. Knopf, 1967), p. 291.

14. Hine, et. al., pp. 58–59, 139.

15. Genovese, pp. 319, 495, 497, 576–577; Hine, pp. 53, 133.

16. Stampp, pp. 177–191; John W. Blassingame, *The Slave Community: Plantation Life in the Antebellum South* (New York: Oxford University Press, 1972), pp. 162–165.

17. Norman R. Yetman, ed., *Voices From Slavery: 100 Authentic Slave Narratives* (Mineola, N.Y.: Dover Publications, Inc., 2000), p. 144.

18. William Cooper, Jr., *The American South, A History*, vol. I (New York: McGraw-Hill, Inc., 1991), p. 242.

19. Ibid.

20. Paul S. Boyer, ed., *The Oxford Companion to United States History* (New York: Oxford University Press, 2001), p. 508.

21. Cooper, p. 151.

22. Ibid., pp. 150–152.

CHAPTER 6. ABOLITION AND EMANCIPATION

1. Alice Dana Adams, *The Neglected Period of Anti-Slavery in America, 1808–1831.* (Williamstown, Mass.: Corner House Publishers, 1973), pp. 83, 93.

2. Benjamin Quarles, *Black Abolitionists* (New York: Oxford University Press, 1969), pp. 3, 54, 59; Darlene Clark Hine, William C. Hine, and Stanley Harrold, *The African-American Odyssey* (Upper Saddle River, N.J.: Prentice Hall, 2003), pp. 104–106.

3. "African Colonization Movement." *The Oxford Companion to United States History*, Paul Boyer, ed. (New York: Oxford University Press, 2001), p. 146.

4. Quarles, p. 17.

5. Adams, 93.

6. Ibid., p. 92.

7. Quarles, p. 180.

8. James M. McPherson, *Ordeal by Fire: The Civil War and Reconstruction*, 2nd ed. (New York: McGraw-Hill, Inc., 1992), p. 44.

9. Frederick Douglass, *Narrative of the Life of Frederick Douglass, An American Slave, Written by Himself, First Published, 1845* (Garden City, N.Y.: Anchor Books, 1963), p. 29.

10. Darlene Clark Hine, *African Americans, A Concise History* (Upper Saddle River, N.J.: Prentice Hall, 2003), p. 129.

11. Darlene Clark Hine, William C. Hine, and Stanley Harrold, *The African-American Odyssey* (Upper Saddle River, N.J.: Prentice Hall, 2000), pp. 182–184.

12. Ibid., p. 197.

13. Ibid., p. 210.

14. Constitution, Article IV, Section 3.

15. Hine, et. al., *The African-American Odyssey*, pp. 200–201.

16. John Hope Franklin, *From Slavery to Freedom: A History of Negro Americans*, 3rd ed. (New York: Alfred A. Knopf, 1967), p. 256; Charles L. Blockson, *The Underground Railroad: First-Person Narratives of Escapes to Freedom in the North* (New York: Prentice Hall, 1987), pp. 2–3.

17. Hine, et. al., *The African-American Odyssey*, pp. 215–216.

18. James M. McPherson, *Battle Cry of Freedom: The Civil War Era* (New York: Ballantine Books, 1989) pp. 88–89; Franklin, p. 266; Geoffrey Ward, *The Civil War: An Illustrated History* (New York: Alfred A. Knopf, 1990), p. 19.

19. James M. McPherson, *Ordeal by Fire: The Civil War and Reconstruction*, 2nd ed. (New York: McGraw-Hill, Inc., 1992), pp. 90–91.

20. McPherson, *Battle Cry of Freedom*, pp. 145–147.

21. Ibid., pp. 152–153.

22. McPherson, *Ordeal by Fire*, pp. 97–98.

23. "Scott v. Sandford," *The Penguin Encyclopedia of American History*, Robert A Rosenbaum, ed. (New York: Penguin Group, 2003), pp. 342–343.

24. McPherson, *Battle Cry of Freedom*, pp. 170–172.

25. Hine, et. al., *African Americans*, p. 160.

26. McPherson, *Battle Cry of Freedom*, pp. 503, 505; Ward, p. 6.

27. Hine, et. al., *The African-American Odyssey*, p. 230.

28. "Confiscation Acts." *The Penguin Encyclopedia of American History*, Robert A. Rosenbaum, ed. (New York: Penguin Group, 2003), p. 87.

29. Hine, et. al., *The African-American Odyssey*, p. 236.

30. McPherson, *Battle Cry of Freedom*, pp. 503, 505.

31. Hine, et. al., *The African-American Odyssey*, p. 238.

32. Hine, et. al., *African Americans*, p. 176.

33. Ibid., p. 177.

34. Franklin, pp. 292–293.

35. Norman R. Yetman, ed., *Voices From Slavery: 100 Authentic Slave Narratives* (Mineola, N.Y.: Dover Publications, Inc., 2000), p. 255.

36. Hine, et. al., *The African-American Odyssey*, p. 259.

✣ G L O S S A R Y ✦

ABOLITIONISM—The political belief that slavery should be abolished, or ended.

BARRACOON—West African open pits which served as holding facilities for slaves to be sold along the coast.

CHOPPING COTTON—Practice of hoeing the weeds in cotton fields.

FACTORS—Men employed by sugar plantation owners to buy slaves as they arrived from Africa.

JUMPER—A white worker who served as an overseer on a plantation. Such a supervisor was to ensure slaves worked by using a whip as punishment.

OUTLIER—An escaped slave who hid out after escape and raided food from nearby farms and plantations.

PANYARINGS—Raiding parties that captured Africans to be sold into slavery.

PATERNALISM—Practice of slave owners of treating their slaves like children.

POPULAR SOVEREIGNTY—Political opportunity allowing the people of a territory to determine whether or not they want to practice slavery.

REFUSE—Slaves who were damaged through illness, malformation, or punishment who would not bring a high price at market.

SCRAMBLE—Slave sale in which potential slave buyers rushed toward a group of pre-priced slaves and selected the ones they wished to buy.

SLAVER—A ship used to transport slaves from Africa to be sold in a slave market.

SUN TO SUN—Working slaves from sunrise to sunset.

FURTHER READING

Blight, David. *The Narrative of the Life of Frederick Douglass: An American Slave.* New York: St. Martin's Press, 1996.

Countryman, Edward. *How Did American Slavery Begin?* Boston: St. Martin's Press, 1999.

Currie, Stephen. *The Liberator: Voice of the Abolitionist Movement.* San Diego: Lucent, 2000.

Diouf, Sylviane A. *Growing Up in Slavery.* Brookfield, Conn. Millbrook Press, 2001.

Harms, Robert. *The Diligent: A Voyage Through the Worlds of the Slave Trade.* New York: Basic Books, 2001.

Haskins, James, and Kathleen Benson. *Building a New Land: African Americans in Colonial America.* New York: HarperCollins Publishers, 2001.

Lester, Julius. *To Be a Slave.* Madison, Wis.: Turtleback Books, 2000.

McKissack, Patricia C. and Frederick. *Days of Jubilee: The End of Slavery in the United States.* New York: Scholastic Press, 2003.

Miller, James, ed. *American Slavery.* San Diego: Greenhaven Press, 2001.

Rappaport, Doreen. *No More!: Stories and Songs of Slave Resistance.* Cambridge, Mass.: Candlewick Press, 2002.

✧ INTERNET ✦ ADDRESSES

"AFRICANS IN AMERICA." *PBS.ORG.* n.d. <http://www.pbs.org/wgbh/aia/home.html>.

"ENCYCLOPEDIA OF SLAVERY." *SPARTACUS.* n.d. <http://www.spartacus.schoolnet.co.uk/USAslavery.htm>.

"THE UNDERGROUND RAILROAD." *NATIONALGEOGRAPHIC.COM.* n.d. <http://www.nationalgeographic.com/railroad/j1.html>.

✧ HISTORIC ✦ SITES

BOSTON AFRICAN AMERICAN NATIONAL HISTORIC SITE
14 Beacon Street, Suite 503, Boston, MA 02108
(617) 742-5415
http://www.nps.gov/boaf/index.htm
boaf@nps.gov

FREDERICK DOUGLASS NATIONAL HISTORIC SITE
1411 W Street SE, Washington, DC 20020
202-426-5961
http://www.nps.gov/frdo/index.htm
NACE_Superintendent@nps.gov

HARPERS FERRY NATIONAL HISTORIC PARK
U.S. Route 340, Harpers Ferry, WV 25425
304-535-6298
http://www.nps.gov/hafe/index.htm
Marsha_Wassel@nps.gov

INDEX

A
abolition, 65, 74, 85, 90
abolitionists, 85, 86, 87, 88
Adams, John, 58
African Methodist Episcopal
Church, 85–86
Alabama, 8, 73, 74, 82, 105
Allen, Richard, 85–86
American Antislavery Society, 90
American Colonization Society, 86
antislavery movement, 87–88, 90,
102
antislavery societies, 66, 87–88, 90
*Appeal to the Colored Citizens of
the World*, 87, 90
Articles of Confederation, 68, 83
Attucks, Crispus, 58–59

B
banjar (banjo), 31, 51
barracoons, 26
Beecher, Lyman, 89
Bell, John, 104
Bethel Church of Philadelphia, 85
"Big House," 48, 50
Bleeding Kansas, 99
Booth, John Wilkes, 111
Boston, 40, 47, 58, 59, 87
Breckinridge, John C., 104
Brooks, Preston, 100
Brown, John, 99, 102–104
Bufford, John 59
Butler, Andrew Pickens, 100

C
Calhoun, John C., 91–92
"call–and–response" singing, 50.
See also slave, music.
Cameron, Simon, 106
Canada, 12, 16, 61
Caribbean, 21, 27, 28, 32–35, 45,
55, 61

Charleston, S.C., 49, 53, 80, 81,
105
Civil War, 56, 82, 105, 106, 111,
112
Clay, Henry, 84
Coffin, Levi, 95
Columbus, Christopher, 18–19, 20
Confederacy, 105, 109
Confiscation Acts of 1861 and
1862, 106–107
Congress, 82, 86, 91, 92, 98, 106,
107, 110
Constitution, the, 92, 101
Constitutional Convention, 67
Constitutional Union Party, 104
Continental Army, 62, 63, 64, 65
Continental Congress, 64, 65
Cornish, Samuel, 85
cotton gin, 70–71
cotton, 70–75

D
Declaration of Independence, 60
Deep South, 62, 82
Delany, Martin, 88
Democrats, 98, 104, 110
Douglas, Stephen, 97, 104
Douglass, Frederick, 88–89, 102,
108, 109
Dred Scott v. Sandford, 100–102
Dutch West India Company, 34–35

E
election of 1860, 104
Elmina, slave fortress, 25
Emancipation Proclamation, 107,
108

F
5th Massachusetts Cavalry
Regiment, 109
55th Massachusetts Regiment, 109
54th Massachusetts Regiment, 108

Finley, Robert, 86
First South Carolina Volunteers, 108
Fort Sumter, 105
Forten, Charlotte, 87
Forten, James, 87
Freedom's Journal, 85
Fugitive Slave Law of 1850, 96

G

Garrison, William Lloyd, 88, 90, 108
Georgia, 47, 49, 54, 64, 69, 105
Graham, Philip, 66
Grandberry, Mary Ella, 80
Great Britain, 53, 58, 59, 68
Grimke sisters, 89

H

Hammond, James H., 77
Harpers Ferry, Va., 102
Hendrick, Caesar, 60
Henson, Josiah, 7–9, 11–17

I

indentured servants, 39, 42
indigo, 69

J

Jackson, Andrew, 91
Jamestown, 39, 41, 69
Jefferson, Thomas, 60
Jones, Absalom, 86

K

Kansas Territory, 98–99, 100
Kansas-Nebraska Act, 98
Kentucky, 68, 82, 84, 93

L

The Liberator, 88, 90
Liberia, 86
Lincoln, Abraham, 103–105, 106, 107, 110, 111
Louisiana, 73, 82, 105
Louisiana Purchase, 82
Louisiana Territory, 84

Loyalists, 61, 69
Lundy, Benjamin, 89

M

manumission laws, 68
Maryland, 7, 8, 9, 40, 43, 47, 54, 55, 65, 66, 67, 68, 88, 93, 95
Massachusetts, 57, 58, 60, 100
Massachusetts General Court, 59
Methodist Episcopal Church, 11
Middle Passage, 28, 46
Mississippi, 73, 74, 82, 105
Mississippi River, 82
Missouri, 82, 83, 84, 93, 98, 101
Missouri Compromise, 81, 84, 92, 98, 101
molasses, 35–36, 45, 47
Monroe, James, 79–80

N

Narrative of the Life of Frederick Douglass, 89
Nebraska Territory, 97–98
New England colonies, 45, 46, 47, 55, 65, 66
Newport, R.I., 46
New York, 43, 52, 55, 65, 66
North Carolina, 65, 87, 105
Northwest Ordinance, 84, 85

O

Old Northwest Territory, 68, 92
Ordinance of 1787, 68, 92

P

panyarings, 26
paternalism, 74
Philadelphia Female Anti-Slavery Society, 87
Phillips, Wendell, 89
Pitcairn, John, 62
Poor, Salem 62
"popular sovereignty," 98
Portuguese slave trade, 18–19, 21, 25–26, 34
Potowatomie Creek, 99

Prosser, Gabriel, 79–80
Purvis, Robert, 88

Q

Quakers, 66

R

Republicans, 104, 110
Revolutionary War, 58, 61, 66, 67
rice production, 47, 48, 69
Ritchie, Thomas, 83
Robinson, Tom, 111
Rolfe, John, 39
rum, 35, 45, 47
Rush, Benjamin, 58
Russwurm, John, 85

S

St. Thomas Episcopal Church, 86
Salem, Peter, 62
Scott, Dred, 100–102
secession, 104, 105
slave,
　buyers, 28
　living conditions, 76–78
　marriages, 42
　mortality, 37, 42
　music, 50
　plantations, 37, 48, 70
　population figures, 38, 43,
　　54–56, 67, 73
　punishments, 37, 51, 78, 81
　rebellions, 52, 53, 79, 81, 87,
　　90
　resistance, 51, 52
　ships, 28–31
　trade, international, 73
　troops during Revolutionary
　　War, 61–63
　women, mistreatment of, 51,
　　78–79
　working conditions, 38, 49, 76
slavery,
　American Revolution and,
　　57–28, 68

British colonial, 21, 26, 28, 34,
　39, 43, 54, 57
importation figures, 21–22, 25,
　38, 43, 56
South Carolina, 43, 49, 52, 54, 64,
　65, 69, 81, 91, 100, 105
Spanish slavers, 34
Stono Rebellion, 53
Stowe, Harriet Beecher, 96–97,
　108
sugar plantations, 19, 20–21,
　35–39
Sumner, Charles, 100
Supreme Court, 101

T

Taney, Roger B., 101
Thirteenth Amendment, 110
Tidewater region, 40, 47, 54, 67,
　93
tobacco, 39, 47, 67, 69
Triangular Trade, 28, 45, 46
Truth, Sojourner, 88
Tubman, Harriet, 93, 95
Turner, Nat, 90, 91

U

Uncle Tom's Cabin, 96–97
Underground Railroad, 92–95
Union, 82, 104, 106
U.S. Senate, 82, 110

V

Vesey, Denmark, 81
Virginia, 39, 40, 41, 42, 47, 52, 55,
　63, 65, 66, 67, 68, 79, 90, 93,
　103, 105
Virginia Negro Codes, 42, 44

W

Walker, David, 87, 90
Washington, Booker T., 112
Washington, George, 60, 61, 62,
　63–64
West Africa, 22, 23, 25
Whitney, Eli, 70–71